CW01514037

IMAC **2021** WIT]
USER GUIDE

A Complete Step By Step Instruction Manual For Beginners And Seniors To Learn How To Use The New iMac Using The M1 Chip Like A Pro With macOS Tips And Tricks

BY

HERBERT A. CLARK

Table of Contents

INTRODUCTION

In April 2021, Apple unveiled its new 24" iMac that has a new design and different colors. The IMac has an M1-based chip created by Apple, replacing the previous Intel chips, bringing for speed and better performance, this is the same chip used in the new MacBook Air, MacBook Pro & Mac mini.

The M1 chip is part of the reasons why the new iMac became thinner, and the device now takes up less space and is easier to move to different locations. It is also more comfortable than the previous version due to the M1 chip's thermal and new cooling system.

M1 IMAC FEATURES

In April 2021, Apple unveiled its new 24 inches iMac with the M1 chip, a vividly designed desktop that comes in different colors.

The IMac features Apple M1-based chip, thereby replacing Intel chips, bringing quick updates and important performance.

Design

The 2021 iMac incorporates a more compact and thinner design than previous iMac models, which was simplified by the performance of the M1 chip. The updated iMac offers a strong performance with a fine design of 11.5 millimeters for a relatively thin profile.

The logic board & thermals that are powered by the M1 chip have been significantly reduced compared to previous generations. The more compact design has reduced the size of the iMac, which will allow the device to take less space and fit easily in more places.

Colour options: This new device comes in seven vibrant colors, such as silver, yellow, blue, purple, orange, and green, allowing customers to choose the right color.

The iMac features softer colors and a thinner border on the front to give the user more attention to the content of the screen, while the back has a darker, more saturated color. To complement the redesigned look, the iMac also has a new power connector that is securely fastened and framed with a 2 -meter colored wire.

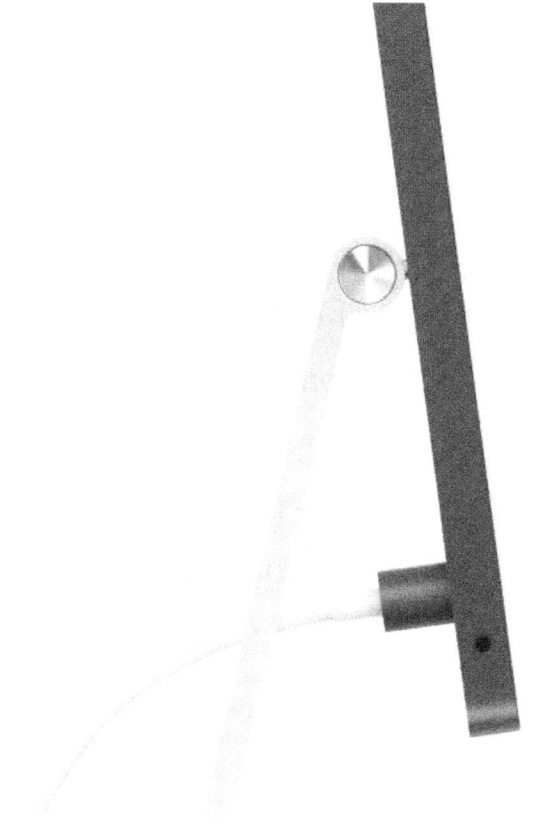

Screen

The new iMac has a 24" 4.5K Retina display with 11.3 million pixels, 500 nit brightness, a wide P3 gamut, and more than a billion colors.

The screen is a bit narrower at the edges and has True Tone technology. In addition, the 4.5K Retina display features Apple's anti-reflective coating.

Port

Each iMac has 2 Thunderbolt ports for fast transfer of data, giving users the ability to connect to most external devices, with compatibility for a 6K external display like the Apple Pro Display XDR. The device configuration with an 8-core GPU provides two extra USB-C ports and also has a 1Gbps Ethernet port in the power adapter, which allows for a smaller desktop.

There's a 3.5mm headphone jack on the left side of the device.

M1 Chip

The new iMac, MacBook Air, MacBook Pro 13, and Mac mini are part of a family of Mac models running on the M1 chip, which is another step away from the Intel chips.

The M1 chip comes with an I/O, RAM, processor, security features, and GPU.

The M1 chip is smaller and more effective than previous Apple chips, with 16 billion transistors.

One of the functions of the M1 is the unified memory architecture. It combines high bandwidth and low latency memory into one pool, which means that the M1 chip technology can access the same data without having to replicate it between memory pools for improvements in performance throughout the system.

Apple says that the iMac offers stronger performance compared to the standard 21.5-inch iMac models

Ram

The M1 iMac, like all other M1 Macs, comes with 8 GB of RAM but can be configured to 16GB Ram with a $200 build to order option.

Storage space

The base model M1 iMacs have 256GB or 512GB of storage space, but customers can configure it to about 2TB of SSD storage.

FaceTime camera

The new iMac features a 1080p FaceTime High-Definition camera. According to Apple, the camera offers high quality and performs great in low-light situations. The iMac also uses the image signal processor on the M1 chip and a Neuron engine, which improves the image quality of the camera with better noise reduction, more dynamic range, and improved automatic exposure & white balance.

Speaker

The iMac has a completely new six-tone sound system. It has two pairs of speakers that improve the bass response by reducing unwanted vibrations. The combined six-tone sound system produces loud and clear bass. The speaker upgrade, as well as Apple's traditional audio algorithms, allows the iMac to be compatible with spatial audio when you play a video in Dolby Atmos for the first time.

Studio Quality Microphone

The new iMac offers a studio-quality three microphone categories for clear calls and audio recording. The microphones are set to reduce the response to the rest of the system, while the lead beacon allows you to better ignore the background sound and focus on the voice of the user.

Magic mouse & magic Trackpad

The M1 iMac is delivered with a new and multi-color Magic Mouse, and customers can choose to add a Magic Trackpad that matches the colour they want.

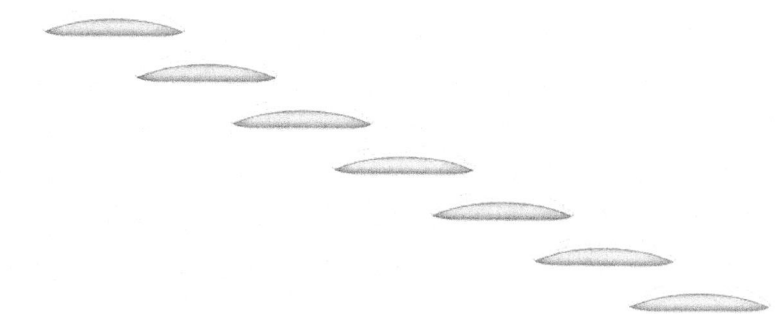

Magic keyboard

The iMac with M1 chip comes with an updated Magic Keyboard that has an updated key structure and more rounded corners.

The biggest change to the design of the new iMac Magic Keyboard is the introduction of the Touch ID to the iMac desktop. Touch ID on the iMac makes it easy to login securely, buy things using Apple Pay, and more.

Customers can pick from 3 Magic Keyboard versions, with options like numeric keyboard & Touch ID.

SETUP YOUR DEVICE

Setup Your New iMac

❖ Press the Power key on your iMac to power it.

❖ Choose any language.

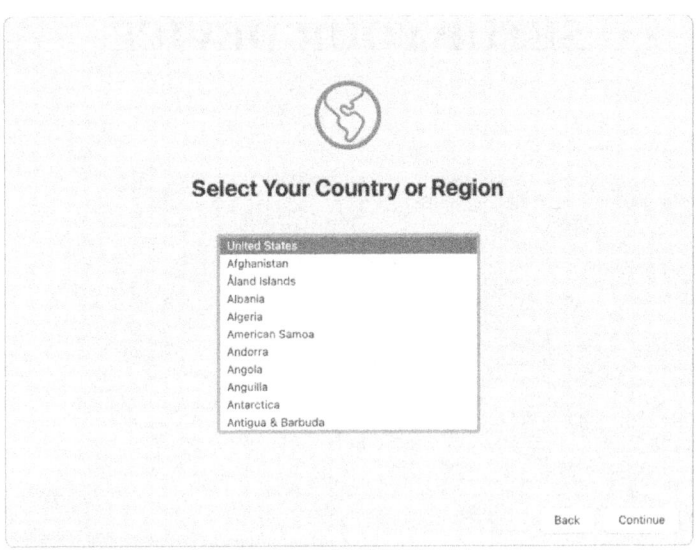

Select Your Country or Region

United States
Afghanistan
Åland Islands
Albania
Algeria
American Samoa
Andorra
Angola
Anguilla
Antarctica
Antigua & Barbuda

Back   Continue

❖ Click the Continue button.

❖ Pick your Wi-Fi network.

   If you want to make use of Ethernet to connect to the Internet, pick other network and pick Ethernet.

❖ If you are making use of Wi-Fi, type your Wi-Fi passcode.

❖ Tap on the Continue button.

❖ If you want to setup your iMac as a new computer, choose do not transfer data now.

❖ Click the Continue button.

❖ Click the box if you to activate the location service on this Mac or you can decide not to. This service is great when using Siri, Maps, Spotlight tips, and more.

❖ Click the Continue button.

❖ Login using your Apple ID.

  • Utilize the Apple ID that you use with your Apple devices to synchronize your services with all services.

  • If you do not own an Apple ID, you can setup one on your device or sign up using an iPhone or iPad.

❖ Click the Continue button.

❖ Click Agree to accept the terms. You can peruse through every segment of the term & condition in more detail.

❖ Press the Accept button to confirm.

❖ Screen time: Monitor and retrieve reports about your computer usage.

❖ Activate Siri and "Hey Siri

- Save files on iCloud: You can store all your content documents, music, photos, movies, and other things in the cloud on iCloud, and you can access them wherever you go.
- Pick an appearance: choose Auto, Dark, or Light for your desktop display.
- Setup the Touch ID: If the keyboard is compatible with it, you can configure the Touch ID when you setup your 24-inch iMac. To configure Touch ID later or add more fingerprints, simply launch System Preferences then tap on Touch ID, and click the Add button and follow the directives on your screen.
- Setup Apple Pay.

FINDING YOUR WAY AROUND YOUR DEVICE

The Desktop

After turning on your device the first thing you see is the Desktop where you launch applications quickly, look for anything on your device and online, arrange files, etc.

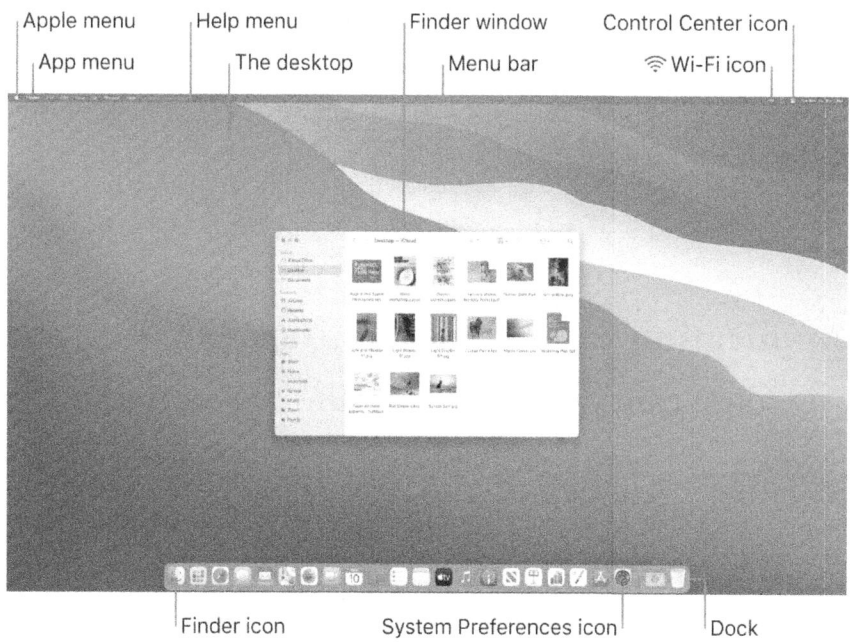

Menu bar: it works at the top of the screen. Use the left menus to select commands and perform tasks in applications. The items on the menu vary depending on the application you are utilizing. Utilize the icons that are on the right to view your Wi-Fi status, connect to a WiFi network, launch the Control Centre, search for things with Spotlight, etc.

Apple menu: The Apple menu features commands used continually and shows in the Top left part of the display. Click the Apple icon to launch it.

Application menu: Many applications and windows can be opened at the same time. The application name is displayed in bold on the Apple menu right side, followed by the menus of the application. When you open another application or click on the window that opens in another application, the name of the application menu would change to that application and the menus in the menu bar also change. If you are looking for a command from the menu and do not find it, check the application menu to see if the application is active or not.

Help menu: Help for the device can be accessed on the menu bar. For help, launch the Finder in the dock, tap on the Help menu and select macOS Help to launch the macOS User manual.

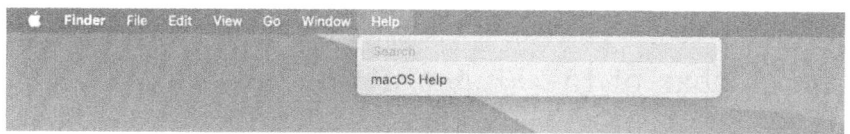

Finder

Utilize Finder to arrange and look for your files. Tap on the icon of the Finder ▟ on the Dock at the lower part of the display to launch the window.

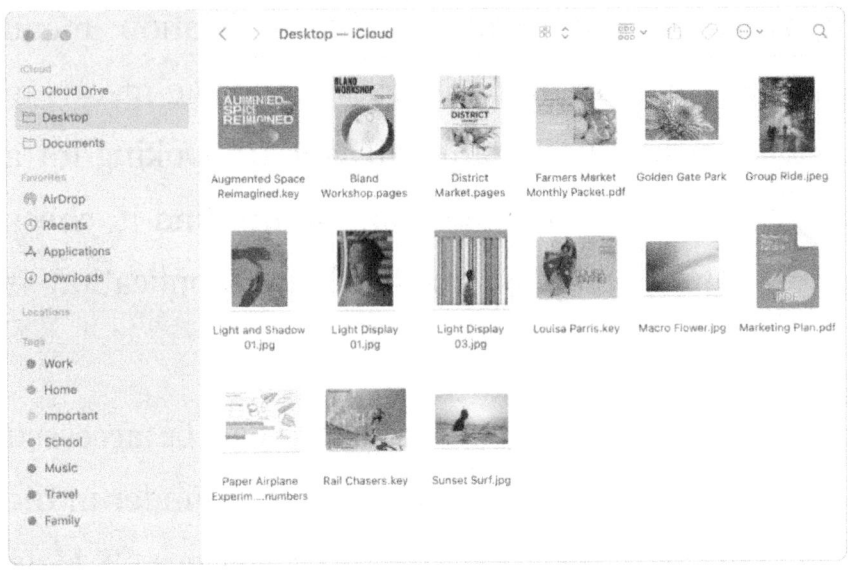

Synchronize devices: When you connect a device, such as an iPad or iPhone, you can find it on the sidebar of the Finder. From this window, you can restore, update, and backup your iMac.

Gallery view

You can get an overview of the file you want, and you would be able to identify your photos, videos, and other docs visually. The preview pane displays info to aid you when identifying the file you want. Utilize the scrubber bar at the lower part of the window to search for what you have in mind. Press Shift-Command-P to conceal or launch the preview pane. To display the file names in Gallery, press Command-J and select **Show File Name**.

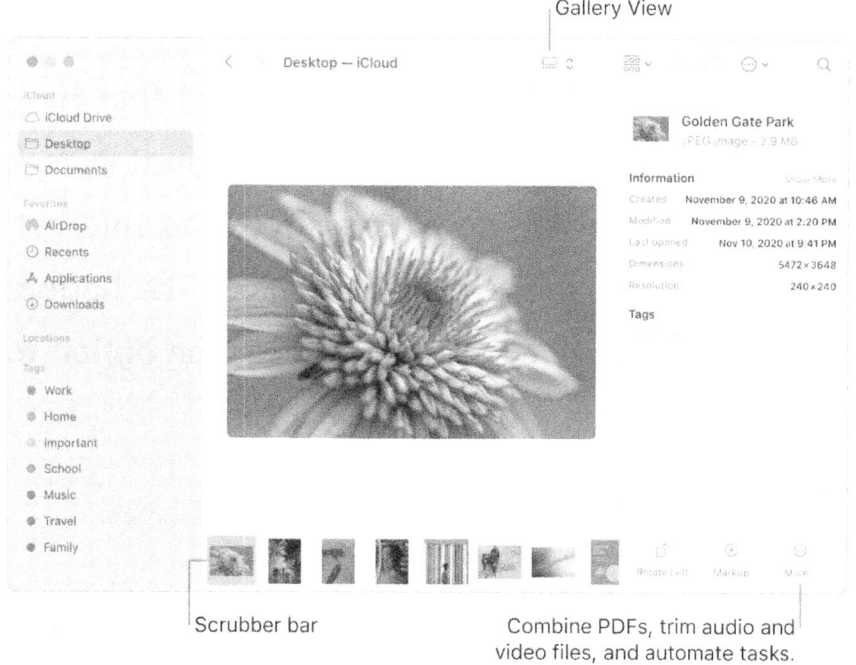

Gallery View

Scrubber bar

Combine PDFs, trim audio and video files, and automate tasks.

The Dock

The Dock is a place where you can easily access applications and features that you are most likely to make use of on a daily basis, such as Launchpad and Trash.

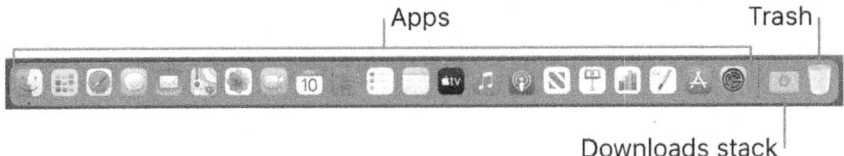

The dock can display three applications that have been used recently and are not already in it as well as a folder for your downloads from the Internet. The location of the Dock by default is the bottom edge of your display, but you can set the option to show it on the left or right side.

Open things on the dock

On the Dock on your Mac, do one of the below:

❖ Launch an application: Click the icon of the application. For instance, on the Dock, tap on the icon of the Finder.

❖ Display an item in the finder: cmd-click the icon of the item.

❖ Go to the previous application and hide the application you are using currently: option-Click the icon of the current application.

❖ Go to another program and hide every other application: Option-command-click on the application icon you want to switch to.

Perform other action on the dock items

On the Dock on your Mac, do one of the below:

❖ Show shortcut menu: ctrl-click an item to show the shortcut menu of the item, then select an action like **Show Recent**, or click on a file name to launch the file.

❖ Force an application to quit: If an application does not respond anymore, ctrl-click the icon of the application, then select Force Quit.

Add, remove, or sort dock items

Do any of the below on your iMac:

❖ Add items to the dock: Drag the applications to the left (or top) of the line separating the newly used applications. Drag files and folders to the right (or bottom) of the screen.

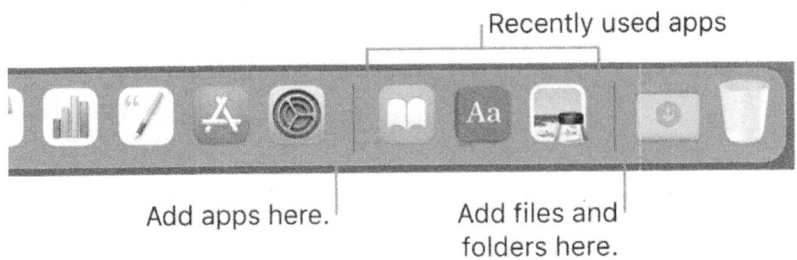

Recently used apps

Add apps here. Add files and folders here.

❖ Remove an item from the Dock: Remove from the Dock by dragging the item out till you see Remove.

If you mistakenly remove an application icon from the dock, it is easy to restore it (the program is still on Mac). Open the application for it to reappear in the dock. Ctrl-Click the icon of the application, and then select Options after that click on Keep in Dock.

❖ Reorder an item in the dock: simply drag any item to another location.

Personalize the Dock

❖ On your Mac, select the Apple menu then click on system preferences..., after that tap on Dock and Menu Bar preferences.

❖ In the "Dock & Menu Bar" segment on the side bar, edit the options you want to.

For instance, you can change the size, and change the location to the left side or the right side of your display.

Click the Help button on the panel to learn about the options.

Notification Center

The notification center has been updated to keep your important info, widgets as well as reminders in a convenient place. Get information about calendar events, shares, weather, etc. - and check for notifications you haven't seen (messages, email, reminders, etc.).

Launch The Notification Center: tap on the time & date at the upper right part of your display.

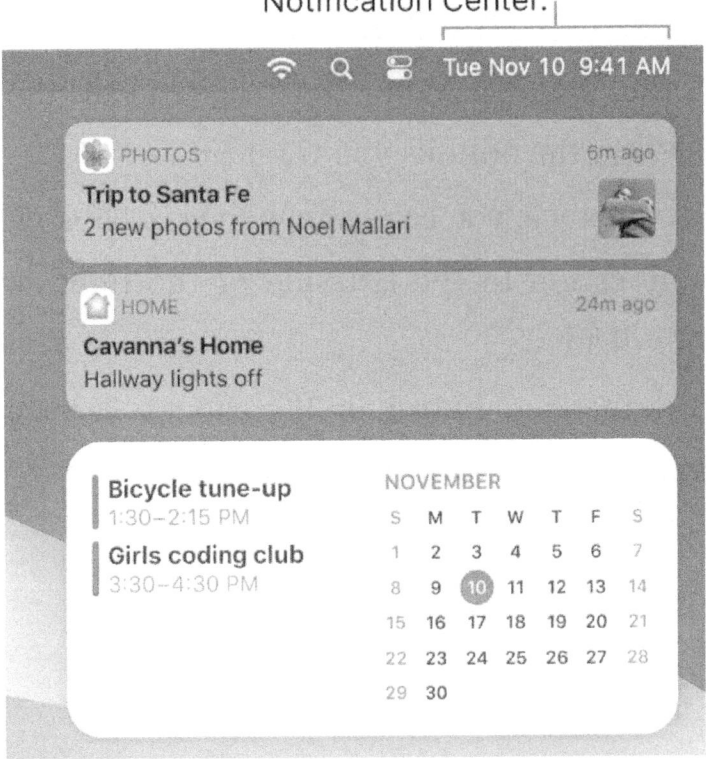

Click to open
Notification Center.

Personalize your widgets: Click on the Edit Widgets button to rearrange, remove, or add widgets. You can also add a third-party widget from the Application Store.

Customize your alert options: Open the network options and click the message to select which message you see. Alerts are periodically sorted, and once-a-day Widgets provide updated updates.

Control center

Click an icon to turn an item on or off.

Open or close Control Center.

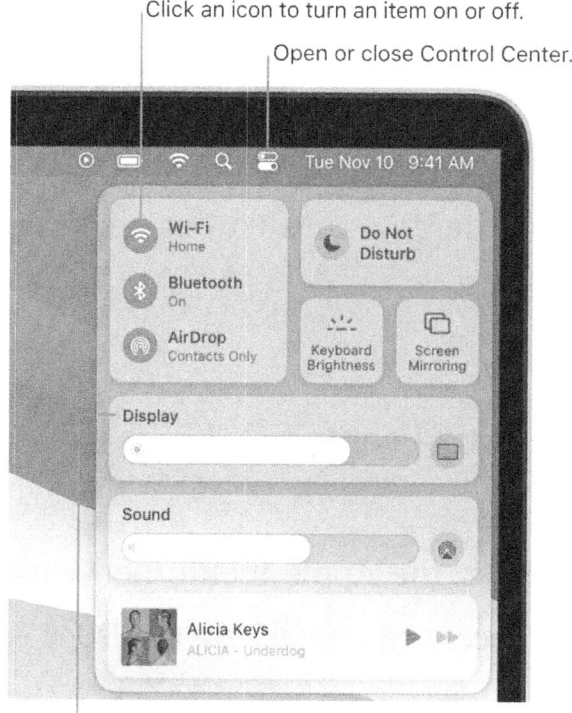

For some controls, click anywhere to see more options.

The iMac Control Center allows you to quickly access important macOS system settings which include DND, Wi-Fi, volume, or brightness. You can personalize the control centre to add other things, like accessibility shortcuts or quick user switching.

How to utilize the control centre

❖ On your iMac, tap on the icon of the Control Center ⚏ on the menu bar.

❖ Drag the slide (like the volume Slide) or click on any icon (like the AirDrop icon). To view other options, click anywhere on an item, or click the arrow ⟩ on the right.

Personalize the control centre

❖ On your iMac, select the Apple menu then click on system preferences.., then click on the Dock & menu bar.

❖ You can click on a segment in the side bar to view items that are always in the control centre or items you can add to the control center.

Control Center: The items in this segment are always displayed in the Control Center; you cannot remove these items.

Other modules: You can add items in this area to the Control Center. Select the item in the sidebar, then check the Show in the Control Center box.

System preferences

The system preferences is where you customize the settings of your device. For instance, Use Desktop and Screen Saver preferences if you want to add a desktop background or select a screen saver.

Personalize your device: select the Apple menu then choose systems preferences, or click the Network preferences icon on the Dock. Then tap the preference type you want to set.

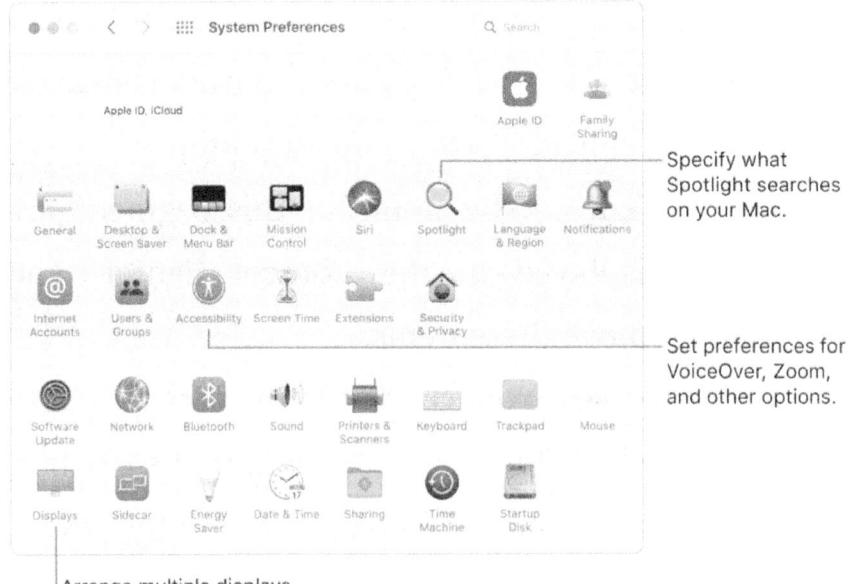

Specify what Spotlight searches on your Mac.

Set preferences for VoiceOver, Zoom, and other options.

Arrange multiple displays, set resolution and brightness, and more.

Update your macOS to the latest version: In Systems Preferences..., click on Software Updates to check if your iMac is using the newest version of the macOS software. You can specify an option for automatic software updates.

Spotlight

Spotlight can assist you when looking for applications, documents, and other files on your iMac quickly. With Siri Tips you can get the most recent news, sports scores, weather report, and much more. Spotlight can even make calculations and convert for you.

Find something

❖ On your iMac, click on the icon of Spotlight ⌕ in the menu bar (if it is displayed), or click on the Cmd-Space bar combination, or press the Spotlight button ⌕ (if there is a keyboard action key)

You can move the Spotlight window anywhere on the desktop by dragging it.

❖ Write what you have in mind on the search field - results will appear when you type.

View search results in Spotlight.

Click a top hit to preview or open the item.

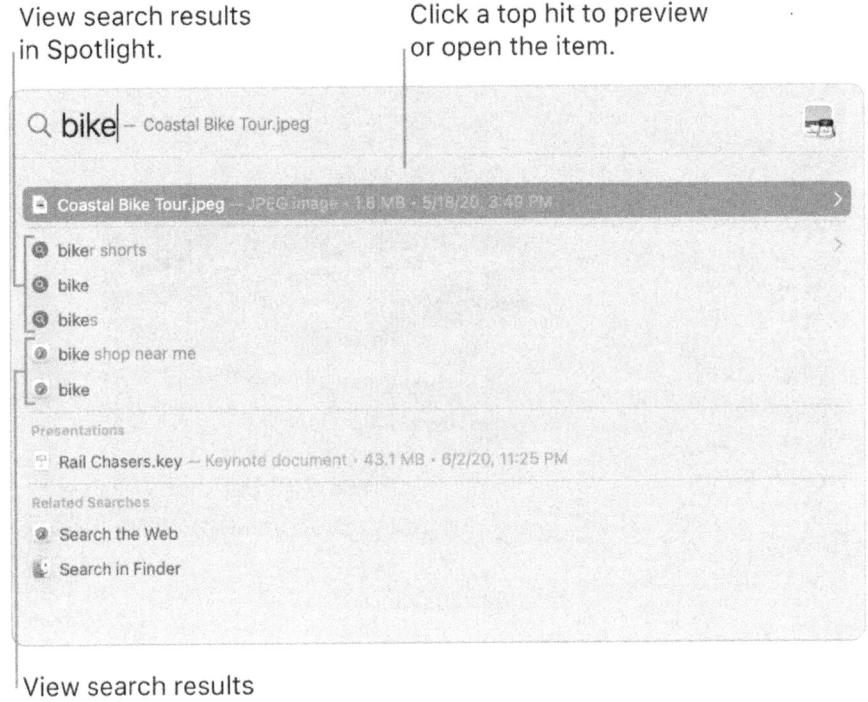

View search results on the web.

Get conversions & calculation in spotlight

You can get currencies converted for you or calculations in the search box by entering measurements, mathematical expressions, temperature, or currency into the Spotlight search box.

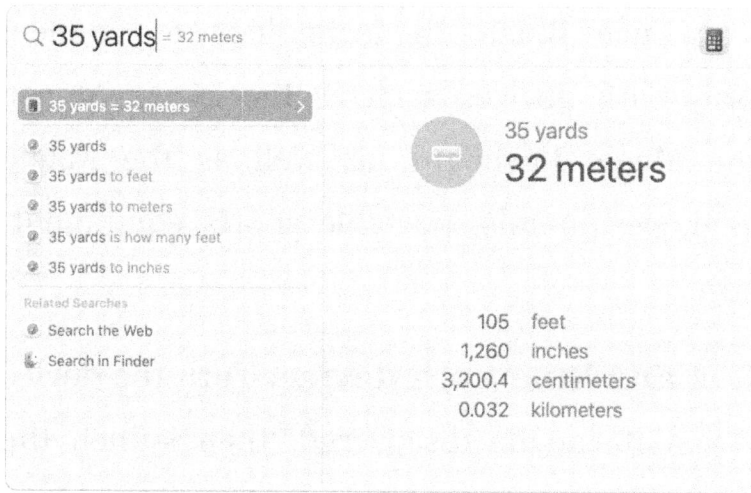

❖ Calculation: type a mathematical expression like 983 + 13.43 or 7420/84.

❖ Converting Currency: type a currency, like $4940, 195 yen, or 590 kroner in euros.

❖ Temperature change: type a temperature, like 67.4F, 93C, or "929K in F".

❖ Measurement conversion: type dimensions such as 74 pounds, 42 stones, or "75 feet to meters".

Tip: In the preview pane, press the Tab key to display additional conversions.

iMAC ACCESSORIES

IMac can use Bluetooth technology to connect wirelessly with devices such as the Magic Mouse and the Magic Keyboard, as well as the Magic Trackpad, peripherals, portable sports equipment, and more.

Connect any Bluetooth device: Turn the device on so that it can be discovered, then launch the System Preferences... and tap on Bluetooth. Pick your device name from the catalog and click on Connect. The device will be connected until it is turned off. Ctrl-Click on the name of the device to disable it.

Turn Bluetooth on or off: Click on the Control Centre logo , then click on the Bluetooth icon , and then press the controls to turn Bluetooth off or on. Your IMac is Bluetooth activated.

Check the battery level: Click on the icon of the Control Center ⚏, click on the Bluetooth icon ✱, and then select your device.

Charge the battery: The magic keyboard and magic mouse has an in-built rechargeable battery.

To charge the device simply connect your magic keyboard or mouse to a flash cable or USB flash drive with the USB-C connected to your iMac.

Magic mouse

You can use the magic mouse anywhere on your computer. If you need to charge or reconnect the mouse, connect a lightning cable or a lightning USB cable to the iMac via USB-C.

Some common actions that can be used with your magic mouse.

Turn the device Off / On: simply Slide the on / off button at the back.

Click: If you want to click or double-click, press on the upper part of the device.

Secondary clicks (for example, right or left click): tap on the left side or right side of your mouse for a secondary click to be performed. (to activate left-click or right-click, head over to System Preferences, then tap on Mouse and select **Secondary Click.**). Or you can press the control button while clicking on the mouse.

Scroll 360°: use one of your fingers to brush to scroll in a page or pan in the direction you want.

Zoom in on the screen: Press and hold the control button and use one of your fingers to scroll so as to expand what is on the screen. (To activate the screen zooming, in System Preferences, tap on Accessibility, click on the Zoom button, and choose

Use a scroll gesture with the modifiers keys to zoom).

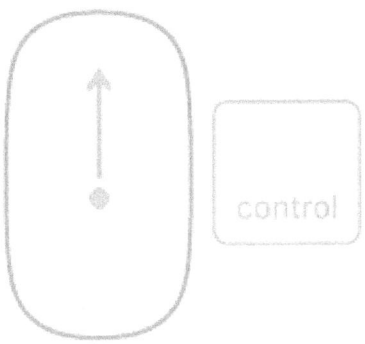

Swipe with two fingers: swipe to the right or left to browse pages, pictures, etc.

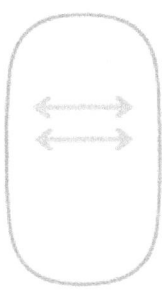

Personalize the mouse gestures: Click on the mouse in System preferences to set preferences like the scrolling and tracking speed and to activate or personalize gestures.

Magic Keyboard with Touch ID

Function (Fn)/Globe key

The included wireless Magic Keyboard for the 24-inch iMac has inbuilt functions that perform many activities, such as entering emoji, changing keyboard language, locking your iMac, and more. The Magic with Touch ID allows you to use a fingerprint to log in and use Apple Pay.

Turn your keyboard on/off: Move the slider at the edge of your device. If your iMac does not accept your keyboard, connect it using the USB-C to lightning cable to pair your iMac with it, and then disconnect the cable and use it without a cable. Utilize the same wire for charging the keyboard.

Lock your iMac: Quickly press the Touch ID or Lock key (there is a lock key for magic keyboards without Touch ID). To unlock the IMac, just press Touch ID or press any button and enter your password.

Setup Touch ID: If you have Touch ID on your keyboard, your fingerprint can be used to open your device and make purchases on the Apple TV, Book Store, Application Store, and sites making use of Apple Pay. You can set it up in the Touch ID pane of Systems Preferences...

Using Touch ID: Gently put one of your fingers on Touch ID. When you restart or start up your device for the first time, you must enter your password to access the iMac. Then, you can use Touch ID anytime your password is needed to open or buy things online.

Configure keyboard options: To set options for Keyboard and Function (Fn) / Globe button, open System Preferences, click on Keyboard, and select options to change the keyboard or input source, display emoji and symbols, start dictation, or function descriptions.

Use emoji or change keyboard languages: Press the Globe button⊕ to move to another keyboard. Press the Globe button⊕ repeatedly to navigate the emoji or other language options specified in the keyboard options, or quickly double-press to begin dictation (if you have configured this option).

Keyboard Shortcuts

You can often do things that require a mouse, trackpad, or other input device by pressing a certain combination of buttons on your keyboard.

To utilize the keyboard shortcut, hold down one of the shortcut button, and then press the last button of the shortcut. For instance, to utilize Cmd-v (paste), hold down the cmd button, then press v, and release both buttons. Mac menus and keyboards often use icons for specific keys, including the toggle key:

- Caps Lock ⇪
- Shift ⇧
- Control (or Ctrl) ^
- Option (or Alt) ⌥
- Command (Cmd) ⌘
- Fn

Some Apple keyboard keys have special functions and symbols like display brightness ☀, keyboard brightness ☼, Mission Control, etc. If these functions are not on the keyboard, you can create your own keyboard shortcuts and recreate some of them.

Common short cuts

❖ Cmd-X: Cut the highlighted item and copy it.

❖ Cmd-C: Copy the items highlighted.

❖ Cmd-V: paste the copied item into the current application or document.

❖ Command-Z: reverse the previous command.

❖ Command-A: highlight all items.

❖ Command-F: look for an item in the document or launch a search window.

❖ Command-H: hide the front application window. Press the Option-Command-H combination to see the front application and hides all other applications.

❖ Cmd-M: minimize the window in the front to the dock.

❖ Cmd-P: Print a doc.

❖ Cmd-S: Save a file.

❖ Command-T: Opens a new table.

❖ Command-W: Close the window.

❖ Opt-Cmd-Esc: quit an application with force.

❖ Cmd- Space Bar: Display or hide the Spotlight search box.

❖ Ctrl-Cmd-Space bar: Display the character viewer for which emojis and other symbols can be selected.

❖ Ctrl-Cmd-F: If the application supports it, use the application in full screen.

❖ Space bar: Utilize Quick View to preview highlighted items.

❖ Command-Tab: move to the other recently used application among the open application.

❖ Shift-Cmd-5: capture a screen shot or screen recording. Or use Shift-Cmd-3 or Shift-Cmd-4 for screen shots.

❖ Shift-Cmd-N: Creates another folder in Finder.

❖ Command-Comma (,): launch the preferences for the front application

Power Shortcuts

You may have to hold down these shortcuts for a longer period. This prevents them from being used unintentionally.

- ❖ Power key: Press to turn on your device or wake up your Mac. Hold down the key for 1.5 secs to sleep your device. * keep holding the button to forcing shut down your device.

- ❖ Opt - Cmd - Power Key: Sleep your Mac.

- ❖ Ctrl-shift-power key: Sleep your mac display.

- ❖ Control-power key: Displays a dialog box asking you if you are going to restart, shut down or sleep.

- ❖ Ctrl - Cmd – Power key: force restart your device without asking to store open and unsaved document

- ❖ Control - Command - Media Eject: close all applications and restart your Mac. If you have any unsaved applications you would be asked to save them

- ❖ Control-Option-Command-Power Button: close all applications and turn off your iMac. If you have any unsaved applications you would be asked to save them

- ❖ Control-Command-Q: instantly lock the screen

❖ Shift-Command-Q: Log out of your macOS user account.

Document shortcuts

❖ Command-B: **Bold** the text that was selected, or turns off boldface on a selected text.

❖ Command-I: *italicize* the text you highlighted, or turn off italic for the highlighted text.

❖ Cmd-K: include a web link.

❖ Cmd-U: <u>underline</u> the text you highlighted or turn off underlining in the highlighted text.

❖ Command-T: display or hide the font window.

❖ Control-Command-D: Display or hide the definition of the highlighted word.

❖ Shift-Command-Colon (:): Displays the spellings & grammar window.

❖ Command-Semicolon (;): look for the words spelled wrongly in a document.

❖ Fn - Up arrow: Top of page: Scroll by one page up.

- ❖ Command - Up arrow: Moves the point of insertion to the document beginning.
- ❖ Command-down arrow: Moves the point of insertion to the document end.
- ❖ Cmd – Left arrow: Move the entry point to the start of the present line.
- ❖ Shift-Cmd-Up Arrow: Select the text at the beginning of the document with the access point.
- ❖ Ctrl-A: Move to the start of the paragraph.
- ❖ Ctrl-E: Move to the end of a paragraph or line.
- ❖ Option-Command-F: Navigate to the search field.
- ❖ Option-Cmd-T: display or hide a tool bar in the application.
- ❖ Opt-Cmd-C: Copy the Style: Copy the settings for the formatting of the selected items.
- ❖ Opt-Cmd-V: paste the copied style
- ❖ Opt-Cmd-I: Display or hide the inspector window.
- ❖ Shift-Cmd-S: Show the Store as dialog box.
- ❖ Shift-Cmd-Minus character (-): Decreases the size of the highlighted item.

❖ Shift - Cmd - Plus (+): Increase the size of the highlighted items.

❖ Shift - Cmd - Question mark(?): launch the Help menu.

CONNECTING IMAC AND OTHER APPLE DEVICES

There are a lot of ways to utilize your iMac with your iPod touch, Apple Watch, iPhone, or iPad. You can move files, edit & share documents, answer calls or sending texts from iMac, etc.

Get access to your contents across your devices:

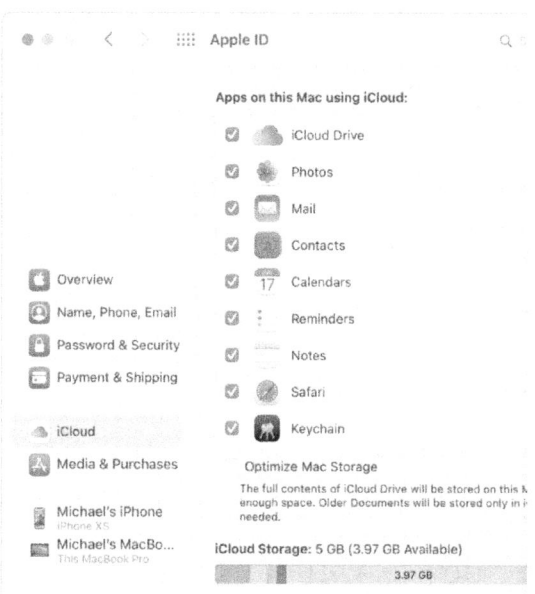

With the help of iCloud, you can save, modify and share your pictures, videos as well as documents to ensure you stay up to date.

If you didn't activate iCloud when setting up your iMac, go to System preferences, tap on Sign In, then log in using your Apple ID or setup a new Apple ID for yourself if you don't own one. Click on iCloud, then activate features you want iCloud to have.

Utilize your Mac with other devices: By making use of Continuity, you can move seamlessly between your Mac and other devices. Simply login with the one Apple ID on each of your devices, and they work together in the right way when your iMac and device are close together.

Handoff

With Handoff, you can begin a task on your iMac, Apple Watch, iPad, or iPhone and then continue it on your other Apple device without having to lose focus on what you are doing. For instance, start to answer a mail on your iPad and finish answering the mail on your iMac. You can utilize hand-off on many Apple applications such as Safari, Pages, Contacts, or Calendar. Some third-party applications may function with Handoff.

Click to continue what you were doing on your iPhone.

To utilize Hand off, Bluetooth, Handoff, and Wi-Fi must also be enabled in systems preferences... (on iMac) and Setting (on your iPadOS and iOS devices). You need to login to all of your Apple devices with one Apple ID.

Activate or deactivate Handoff

If you do not see the Handoff option on your device, it will not work with Handoff.

❖ On your iMac

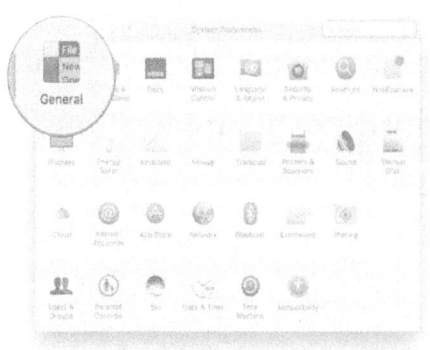 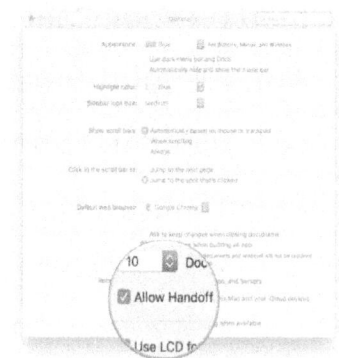

Select the Apple menu🍎 and click on General
after that select **Allow hand off between this
iMac and your iCloud device** (at the lower
part of the pane). If you want to deactivate it
simply unselect it.

❖ On your iPod touch, iPhone, or iPad: launch the
Settings application, click on General then tap on
AirPlay and Handoff, after that activate Handoff.

❖ On the Apple Watch: launch the watch
application on your iPhone head over to the my
Watch segment then click on General after that
activate or deactivate Handoff.

Handoff between your devices

❖ From your iMac to your iPadOS or iOS device

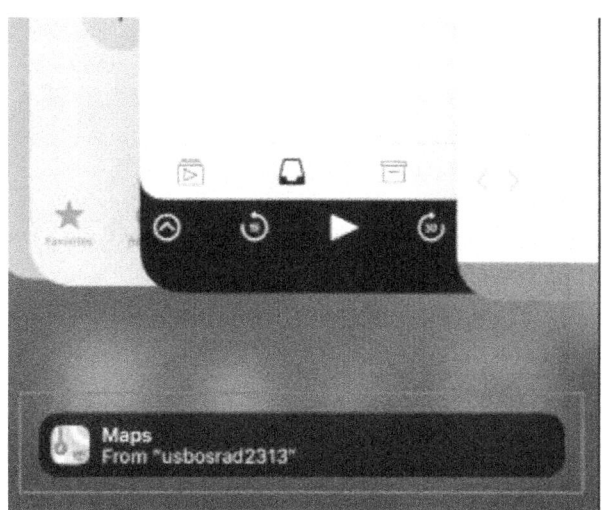

The Hand off icon of the application you are making use of on your iMac would show up on your iPhone (at the lower part of the application switcher) or on the iPod touch or iPad (at the dock end). Click on it to continue working on the application.

❖ From your iOS device or from your iPadOS device or Apple Watch to your iMac: The hand-off icon of the application you are making use of would show up on the far right of the Dock (or below, depending on where the Dock is located). Click on the icon to continue working on the application.

You can press Command-Tab to change to the app that has the Hand off icon.

Universal Clipboard

You can copy text, pictures, & videos from one of your Apple devices and paste them into another Apple device using Universal Clipboard, For instance, you can copy a certain recipe from your iPad and paste the recipe on your iMac near you.

To use a Universal Clipboard, Wi-Fi, Bluetooth, and Handoff must be activated on your device in System Preferences (iMac) and Settings (on your iOS devices and iPadOS devices). You have to login using one Apple ID on your devices.

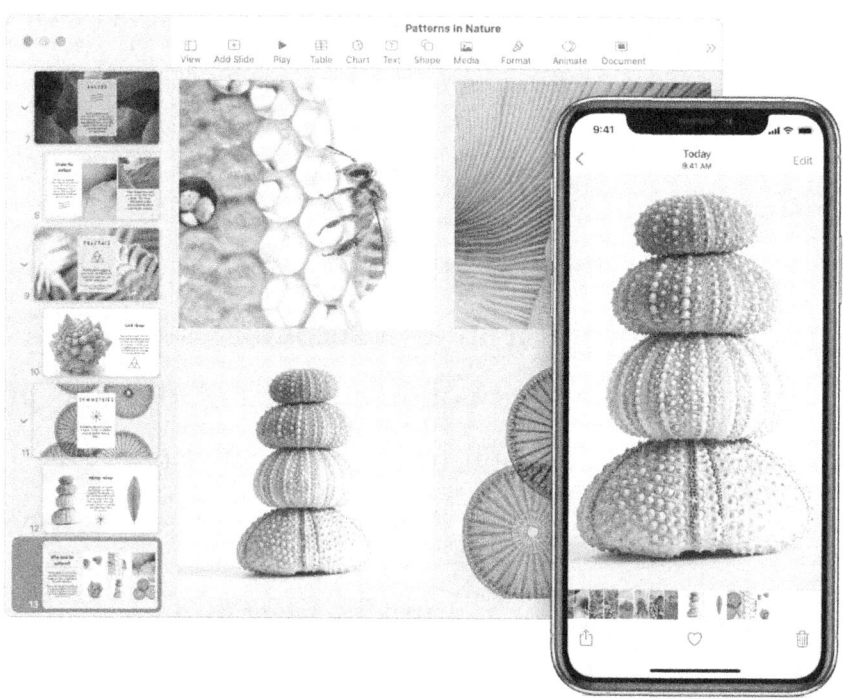

❖ Copying from a device: highlight the items you plan to copy. For instance, press the Command-C combination on your Mac keyboard or select Edit and then tap on Copy.

Copied content will be available on your other devices for a limited time.

❖ Pasting on your other device: hover your cursor to where you want to paste the copied items and paste it. For instance, tap your iPad display twice and tap on paste.

Sidecar

Rather than limiting the desktop to the iMac, making use of the iPad as a secondary monitor for all Macs provides a ton of extensions. iPad users can utilize an Apple Pencil to sketch and connect with iMac applications using Sidecar in a whole new way.

Sidecar is a built-in feature in macOS and iPadOS that allows users to have the two devices connected wirelessly. When paired, the iPad becomes the second screen of the iMac; you can shift applications to an iPad and orient them to your iMac screen, like any external monitor.

Best of all, you can use the iPad app when you run Sidecar on the iPad. The second screen scenario for the iPad doesn't limit what you can do with Sidecar on the iPad.

You can utilize sidecar in iPads that are compatible with Apple pencil and work with iPadOS 13 or after

Prerequisites for using Sidecar

- Ensure that your iMac and iPad are signed in with one Apple ID
- Bluetooth needs to be turned on

- Make sure the two devices WiFi network are active
- Make sure your Mac and iPad are fully charged or plugged in.
- Place both devices in a 10 feet range

Setup Sidecar on iMac

❖ Select the Apple menu

❖ Click on System Preferences...

❖ Select Sidecar

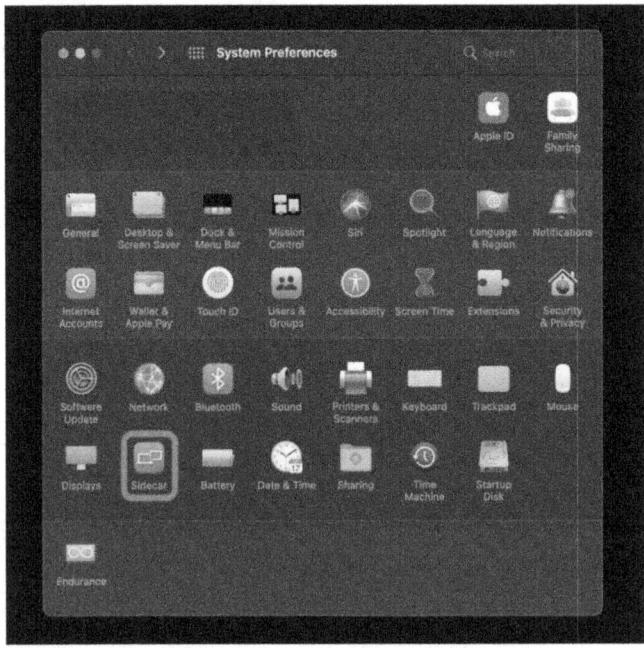

❖ Select the iPad you want to connect to and the settings you want

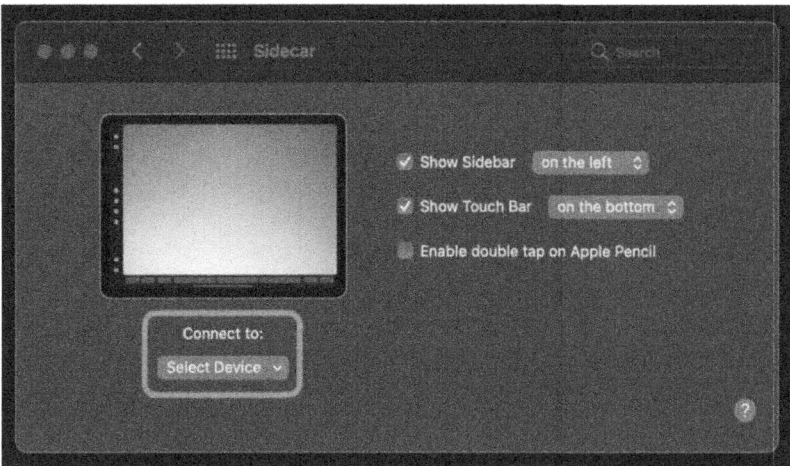

Now the connected iPad will be the second display for the Mac.

You can click on the control centre icon. Tap on Screen Mirroring⬓, and then pick the device you want to connect to.

Use Sidecar

After connecting your iMac and your iPad do any of the below:

❖ Shift windows from your iMac to your iPad: Drag the window to the edge of your iMac screen till the cursor shows up on the display of your iPad. Otherwise, when you making use of an application, select Window then click on Move Window to the iPad.

❖ Shift window from the iPad to your iMac: Drag the window to the edge of your iPad display till the pointer is on your iMac. Alternatively, When you making use of an application, select Window then tap on Move windows back to iMac.

❖ Utilize the side bar on your iPad: click on some icons in the sidebar to display ⎘ or conceal ⎗ the side bar menu bar, display ⎖ or conceal ⎘ the dock, or show the on-screen keyboard ⌨ using your fingers or Apple Pencil. Otherwise, use one or more modifiers such as Control ⌃ to utilize keyboard shortcuts.

❖ Use Apple Pencil on iPad: Click to select menu, items like files, check boxes, menu commands with your Apple Pencil. If Apple Pencil is compatible with it (and if you select this option in the Sidecar option), you can tap the lower part of the Apple Pencil two times to change the drawing tool in certain applications.

❖ Move between iPad & iMac Desktop on your iPad: Swipe using a finger up from the bottom of the iPad to show the home screen. Swipe up and stop at the middle of your iPad display to show the iPad Dock. To go back to the iMac desktop, Swipe up and click on the Sidecar icon .

When you want to stop making use of your iPad, click the disconnect logo on the lower part of your iPad display.

Continuity Camera

The Continuity Camera feature allows you to take pictures or scan documents on an iPhone or iPad and send them to your iMac immediately.

To be able to utilize Continuity Camera, you would need an iOS 12 or after device, or an iPadOS 13 or after device

Both iMac and mobile devices should have their Wi-Fi and Bluetooth Turned on, and should be logged in with one Apple ID.

Several applications are compatible with continuity camera:

- ❖ TextEdit
- ❖ Pages
- ❖ Mail
- ❖ Finder
- ❖ Message
- ❖ Notes
- ❖ Numbers
- ❖ Keynote

How to use the continuity camera feature

You can take a photo and scan documents with Continuity Camera

Taking a photo

❖ If you are importing images into applications like Mail, Notes, Messages, select files while if you are using keynote, pages, etc, simply right-click or ctrl-click on the place you want the image to appears.

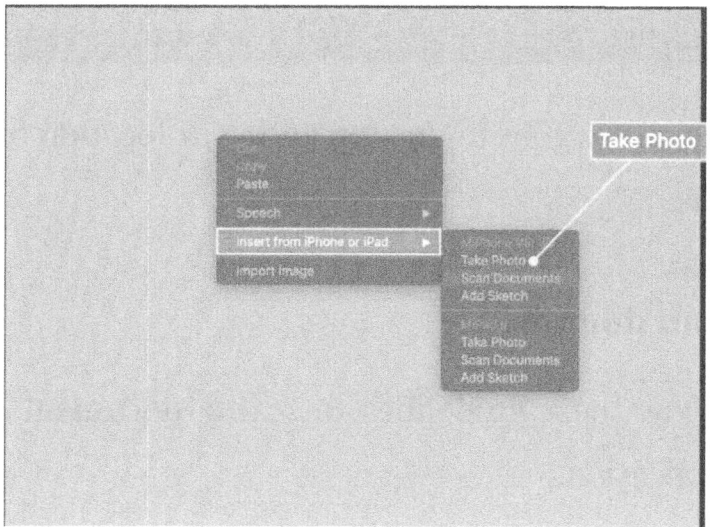

❖ From the menu that shows up, click on the **Import from iPad or iPhone** button and choose **Take Picture**. You may have to choose

the **take photo** option under iPadOS or iOS device before taking the picture

❖ Take the picture on your iPad or iPhone and click on Use picture or you can take on retake if you do not like the picture.

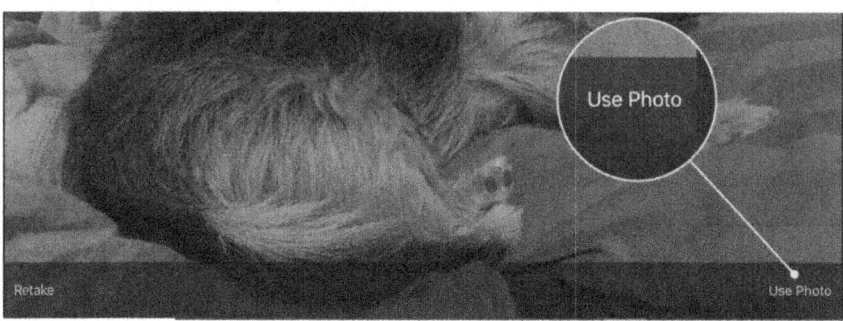

The image goes to the app and your location on your iMac.

Scan document

Follow these guidelines to scan a document in any application.

❖ If you are scanning documents into applications like Mail, Notes, Messages, Choose files while if you are using keynote, pages, etc, simply right-click or ctrl-click on the place you want the image to appears.

❖ From the menu that shows up, click on the **Import from iPad or iPhone** button and choose **Scan Documents**. You may have to choose the **scan document** option under iPadOS or iOS device before scanning the documents

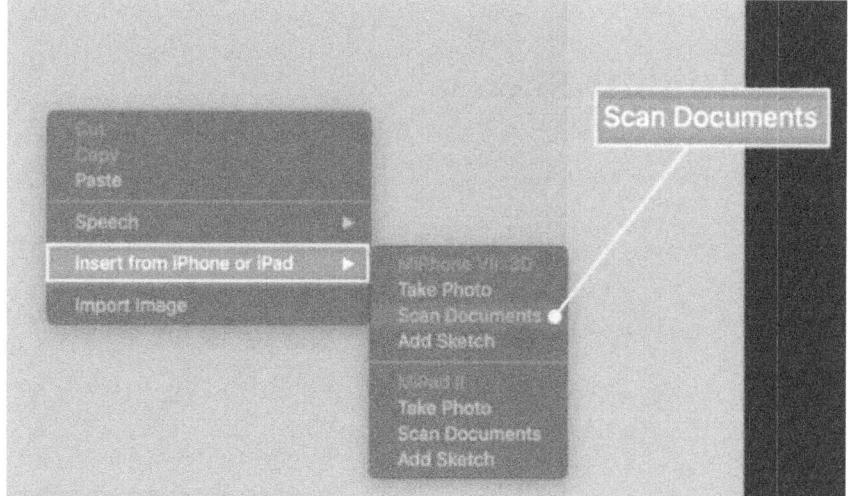

❖ Make sure the camera is facing the document you want to scan with your iPhone or iPad - the device will scan the document automatically when the view is clear. You can also manually

scan the document by clicking on your iPhone or iPad capture button.

- ❖ If necessary, drag the corners around the document to adjust the cut.
- ❖ Scan again if necessary. Once done, tap on **keep scan**
- ❖ The document is transferred to the application on your iMac.

Continuity Sketch

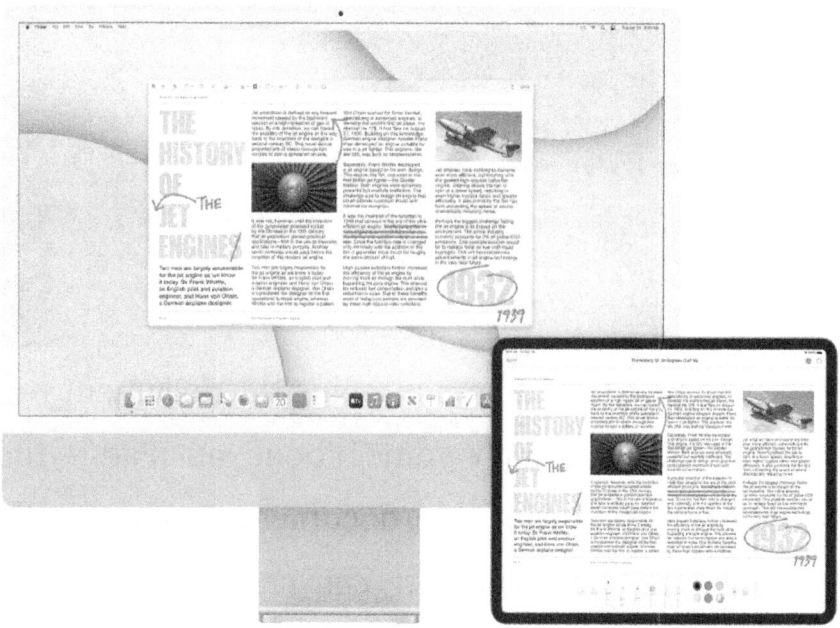

You can make a sketch with your iPad or iPhone and have it show up immediately on your iMac where you really need it, such as a message, a folder, an e-mail, a document, or a note.

To use this feature, your device must have Wi-Fi and Bluetooth activated

- Place the pointer where you want the markup or sketch to be. For instance, in documents, notes, or e-mails.
- Select File then click on insert from iPad or iPhone, then select Add sketch.
  You can also Ctrl-click the desktop or folder in a Finder window, select Import from your iPad or iPhone, and then select **Add Sketch**.
  If you do not see the commands in the File menu, it may be in another menu (like the Edit menu or the insert menu) or the application you are making use of may not be compatible with them.

- On your iOS device or iPadOS device, draw a sketch with your finger or with the Apple Pencil on your iPad.
- When you're ready, press the done button.
- The sketch will appear where you placed the pointer, or if you start with your desktop or folder on your Mac.

AirDrop

Control who can
send items to you.

AirDrop allows you to send docs, pictures, map location, web pages, etc. to a nearby iPad, iPhone, or Mac wirelessly.

Send things with AirDrop

With AirDrop on your iMac, you can send things from the Finder, desktop, or applications like Safari or Maps.

❖ From a Finder window or the desktop: ctrl-click what you want to send, select Share then tap on AirDrop from the menu, and then choose the device you are sending the item to.

❖ From the Finder: tap on AirDrop in the side bar of the Finder, after that drag the item to the apple device you are sending the item to.

❖ From an application: click the share button ⎙ on the tool bar of the application, select AirDrop, and choose the device you want the item to be sent to.

Receive with AirDrop

When a person sends you an item with AirDrop, you can decide whether to receive it or not.

AirDrop makes use of Wi-Fi & Bluetooth to send items between devices. Your Mac may already have Wi-Fi & Bluetooth activated. Otherwise, you would be told to activate it when you try to send something.

❖ Accept the item in the menu that opens with AirDrop notifications on your Mac, and then select an option.

If someone wants to send you a file but cannot see your iMac, ensure you have set it up so others can send things to you via AirDrop.

Let others send things to your iMac via AirDrop

❖ In the Dock, tap on the Finder icon to open the Finder window on your iMac

❖ Click AirDrop in the side bar of Finder.

❖ Then click on the **Allow me to be discovered by** button and select an option in the window that opens.

Use the Control Center to control AirDrop

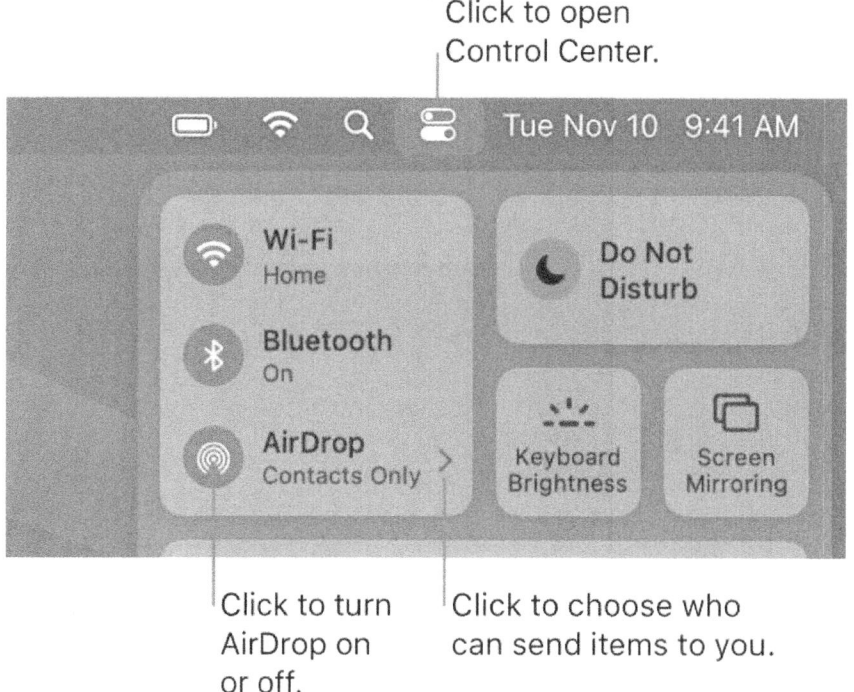

Click to open
Control Center.

Click to turn
AirDrop on
or off.

Click to choose who
can send items to you.

You can use the Control Center to activate or deactivate AirDrop quickly and choose who can send it to you via AirDrop.

On your iMac, click on the Control Centre, then do one of the below:

❖ Enable or disable AirDrop: tap the AirDrop icon.
❖ Select people that can send things to you: tap on the arrow beside AirDrop, then tap on everybody or Contacts.

AirPlay

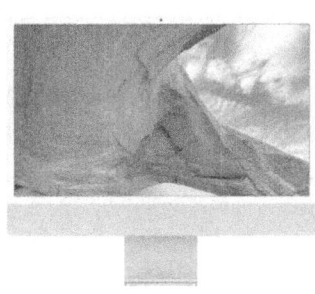 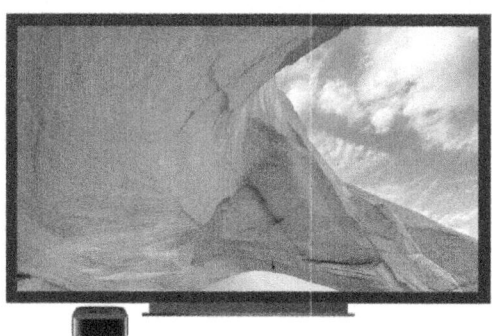

Display what's on your Mac on the big screen with AirPlay. If you want to mirror your Mac on a TV screen or utilize the HDTV as a secondary screen, ensure that the Apple TV is on one Wi-Fi with your Mac.

Mirror the desktop: open the Control Centre on your iMac, tap the Screen Mirror screen icon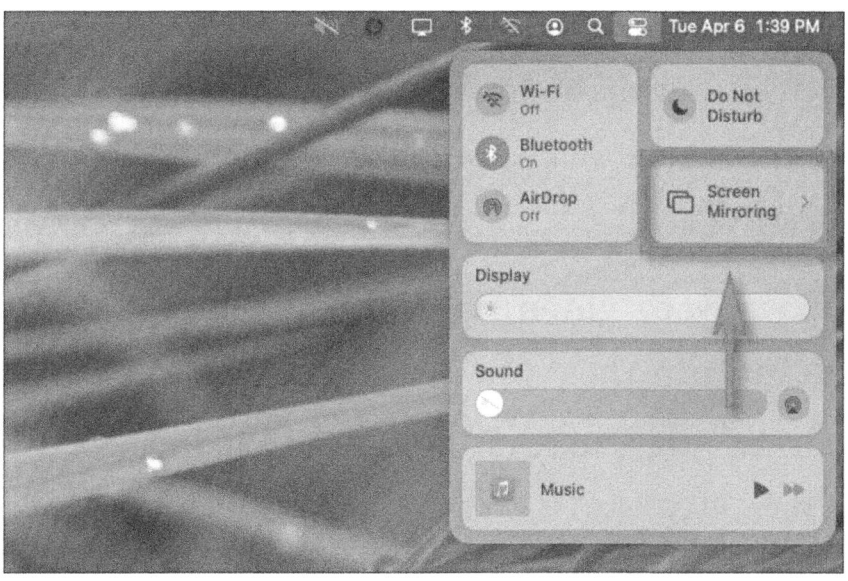, and select the Apple TV. While AirPlay is running, the icon is blue.

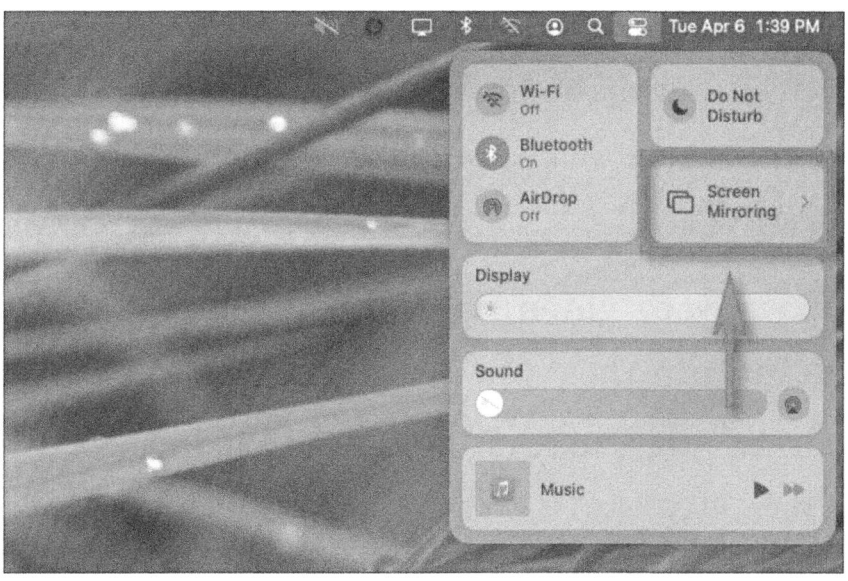

Whenever you want, click on the Screen Mirror icon to see the connection status, or to switch from mirror mode to the **Use as separate display** mode

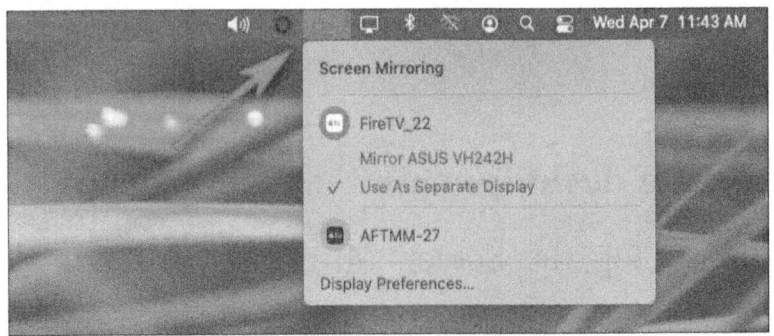

If you want to stop connecting and sharing the screen, click the Screen Mirror icon (or click the Screen Mirror button in the Control Center) and click on the name of the receiving device that displays in blue.

Play web video without displaying your desktop: When you see a web video with the AirPlay icon, click on the icon and choose the Apple TV.

Tip: If the image does not fit your HDTV display after projecting the display simply resize the desktop size. Click on the AirPlay icon in the video, and then select any option in the **Match Desktop Size To** section.

ESSENTIAL SETTINGS

Take a screenshot or screen record with screenshot

You can take a screenshot or record your iMac display using screenshot. Screenshot provides a number of tools that would allow you to easily record videos, and take screenshots with control options, such as setting a timer delay or adding clicks or the cursor.

❖ On your keyboard press, the Shift-Command-5 combination to open screenshot and show the tools on your iMac.

❖ Tap on any of the options to use it to select what you want to snap or record.

For a part of your display, drag the frame to change the size of the image.

Take a picture of the whole screen

Take a window

Take part of the screen

Record the whole display

Record a part of the display

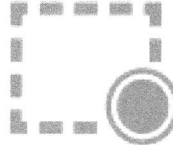

❖ If you want, click Options.

❖ Start a screenshot or record:

- For the whole display or part of it: Tap on Capture.

- For a window: hover the cursor to that window, and tap on it.

- For a screen record: Click on record. To end the recording, click on the end icon⊙ on the menu bar.

- Then save it

Take photos with keyboard shortcuts

You can use different keyboard shortcuts on your iMac to take screenshots. Files are stored on the desktop.

❖ Take a picture of the whole display: Press the Shift-Cmd-3 combination.

- ❖ Take part of your display: Press Shift-Cmd-4 combination, then move the pointer to where you want to begin the screenshot. Press the button on the mouse, drag where you wish to snap, and release the mouse.

- ❖ Take a window: Press the Shift-Cmd-4 combination, after that press the spacebar. Hover the camera cursor around the window or menu bar to highlight the camera screen, then click.

- ❖ Snap menu items and a menu: Open the menu, then press the Shift-Cmd-4 combination, and then drag the cursor over the items of the menu you want to capture.

- ❖ Open a screen shot: Press the Shift-Cmd 5 combination on your keyboard.

You can personalize these keyboard shortcuts on your iMac, simply select the Apple menu then tap on system preferences..., click on Keyboard, and click on shortcut.

Save space on IMac

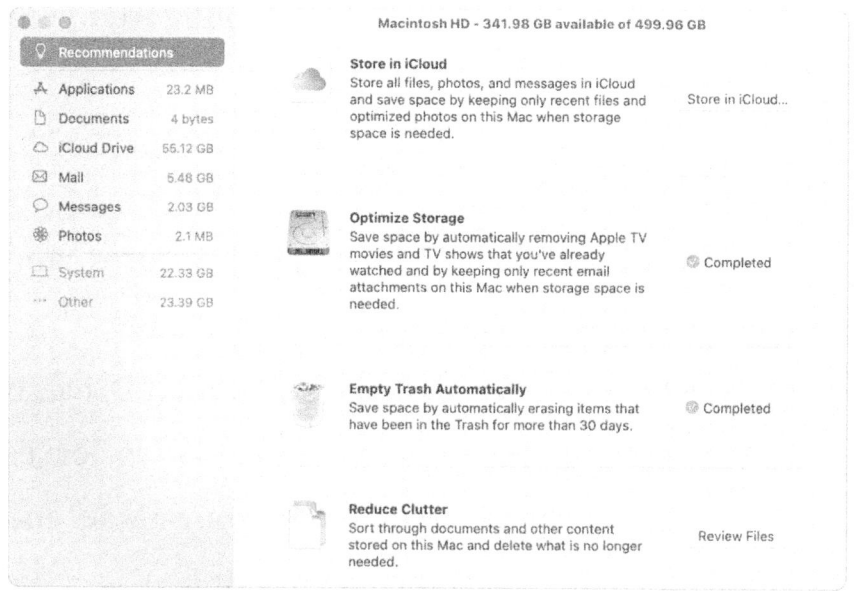

With Optimize Storage, you can free space automatically by making files available only when needed. Your oldest files will be saved on iCloud and IMAP e-mail or exchange server so that you can download them anytime. Tools are also available for identifying and deleting large files.

Optimize storage: To view the storage suggestions, click on the Apple logo then click on

About this Mac, click on Storage, after that click on the Manage button. You will see different suggestions depending on how you configured your iMac.

Make choices to:

❖ Save in iCloud: Save all messages, pictures, and files to iCloud and save space on your iMac.

- Desktop and files: Save files to iCloud Drive. If you need storage space, iCloud Drive leaves the files opened recently on your iMac and provides the oldest files on demand.

- Pictures: Save photos and videos to iCloud Photos. If you need storage space, iCloud Photos uses optimal versions of the pictures and videos on your iMac and provides the original if needed.

- Messages: Save all messages in iCloud. If you need storage space, iCloud leaves the latest attachments on your iMac and provides the oldest on demand.

- ❖ Optimize storage: Optimize storage for movies and TV shows in the Apple TV application and save space on your iMac. You can decide to remove TV shows or movies from your iMac immediately after watching them.
- ❖ Automatic Empty Trash: Automatic removal of items in the trash for above 30 days.
- ❖ Reduce Clutter: identify large files easily and delete unnecessary files. To view more files, click on the categories in the sidebar which include Trash, Documents, Photos, Mail, iCloud Drive, Music Creation, Messages, Books, etc.

To help save space when you are working:

- ❖ Safari prevents you from downloading a file twice
- ❖ macOS notifies you to remove the installer software after you install a new application
- ❖ macOS clears caches & logs that can be removed when you have low storage space

Calendar

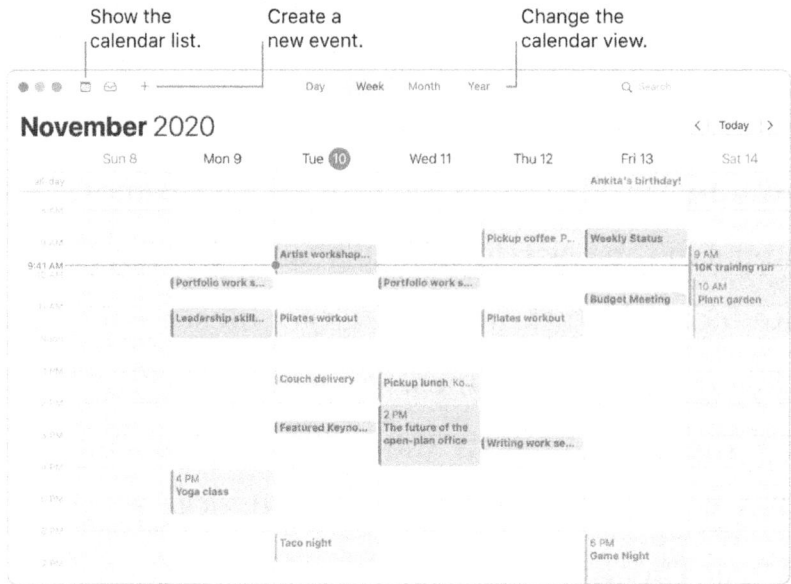

Create multiple calendars to help track your busy schedule and manage them all in one place.

Create event: Tap on the Add button + to add another event. Click on an event twice to invite someone, then tap on the Add invitees segment, and enter an email address. The calendar would tell you when the invited people respond.

Tip: After adding a location to your event, your calendar displays a map, time to move, weather information, and more.

Calendar for all aspects of your life: Create special calendars like school, work, and home, each with its own color. To create a calendar, select File> New Calendar, and ctrl-click each calendar to select a new color

Mail

Mail allows you to manage all your email accounts from one application.

Add an email account to use mail

❖ The first time you launch the Mail application on your iMac, you may be asked to add an account. Choose an account type - if you do not see the type of email you make use of, choose the **Other**

Mail Account option, then enter your account details.

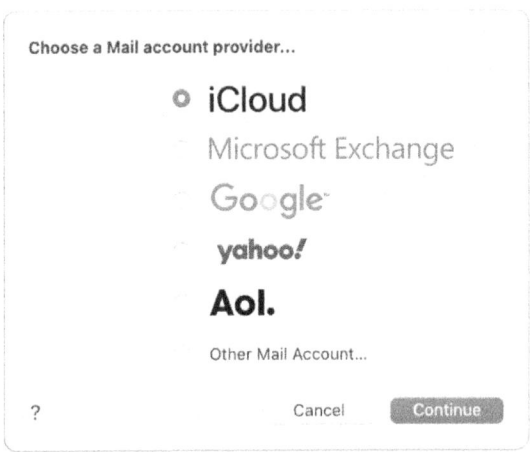

❖ If you added an email account already, you can add more. In the Mail application, select Mail> Add account, choose the account type, and then enter your account details. Ensure the check box for the Mail is selected for the account.

Remove an email account

When you delete an email account, you delete the account messages and they are no longer on the iMac. A copy of the message remains on the account's email server and is still available

- ❖ In the Mail application on your iMac, select Mail> preferences..., and then click on Accounts.
- ❖ Choose an account, then tap on the Delete icon ⎯ .

Search for a message

Write in the search box to view tips on the most relevant messages for your search.

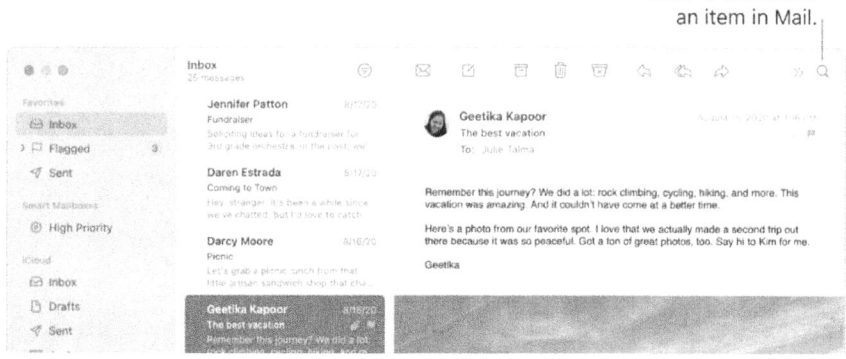

Click to search for an item in Mail.

Customize any message

Add emoji or images with just one click. Select photos from the photo library or take them to your iPhone or iPad.

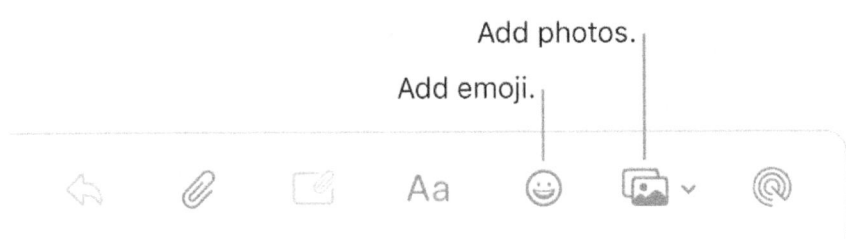

Add photos.

Add emoji.

Never forget email: Check the mail application icon in the Dock to view the number of messages you have not read. When you receive a new email, a notification shows up on the upper-right side of your display for a quick preview of incoming messages.

You have unread messages.

Notes

Notes are not just for text. Write a quick thought, or add a check list, photos, weblinks, etc. Shared folders allow a whole folder of notes to be shared into a group, and anyone can participate.

Tip: When you sign in using your Apple ID and enable iCloud for Notes it will be updated on all of your Apple devices, which means that you can create a list on your iMac, and check it on your iPhone.

Personalize your tool bar: Right-click anywhere in the toolbar to launch a custom window. Drag the items you want into the toolbar for easy access.

Attach webpage previews, files, map locations, etc.

❖ To add videos, pictures, and more to a Note, do any of the below:

Note: If you choose any Locked note, you will not be able to add video, audio, PDF, or files.

- From the desktop: simply drag the file into the note.
- From Photo Library: drag the picture from the photos library to the note.

- From other applications, such as Photos, Safari, Maps, etc: click on the Share icon, then select Notes.

To resize the image, scanned document, or PDF file in the note, ctrl-click on it, then select view as small image or view as large image.

Add to the table: Click the Spreadsheet icon to add a spreadsheet to your notes

Lock a note: You can create a passcode to lock a note you do not want someone else to have access to. To set a passcode, select Notes> preferences...., and click on the Set Passcode button. To lock a note, choose the note then select File and click on Lock note.

Pages

Utilize the Pages application to create media-rich documents and books on your iMac. Launch and edit Microsoft Word files.

The Pages application has professional templates ready to use for books, newsletters, reports, resumes, and more that make it easy to get started with your project.

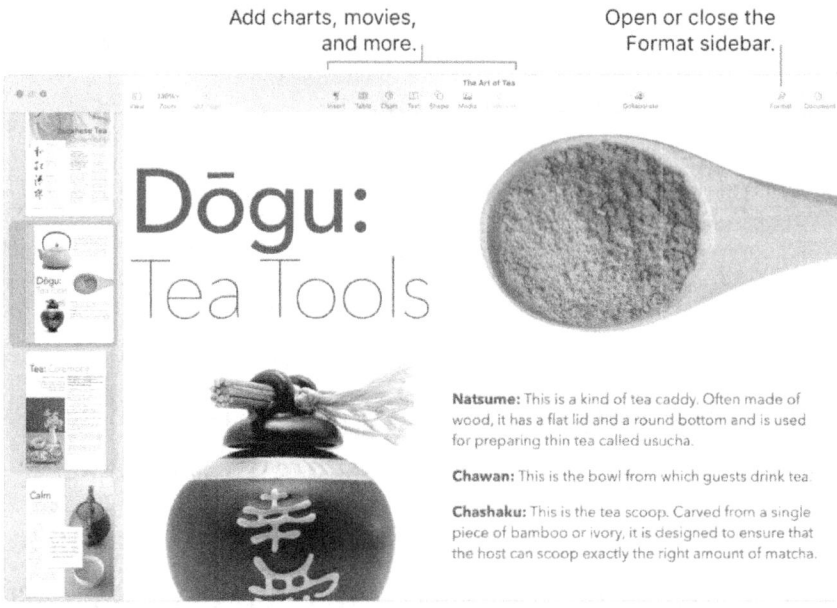

Add charts, movies, and more.

Open or close the Format sidebar.

All your tools for formatting in one place: Click the Format icon on the tool bar to launch the Format Inspector. Choose any item in the doc and the option to edit it will show up.

The text rotates around the image: When you paste an image into a document, the text automatically rotates around the image. You can configure how the text is covered on the Format sidebar.

Lore feum quisciliqui ting eugait ullandignim zzrit iriustrud doluptat volum il il iustin utet, sum dolore tat volobor autpat alisim quipis nit iure vendrerit eugait ing et ad magnim amconse min ulla corper in heniat accum am dipit lutatuero od. Aute duisim zzriusto elit illut nismodo uptat, quis am veliquisi. Lor sequis augait lam vel del ullan velis nulputet utat dit nonsed tionsequat.

Move a graphic into a text block...

Lore feum quisciliqui ting eugait ullandignim zzrit iriustrud doluptat volum il il iustin utet, sum dolore tat 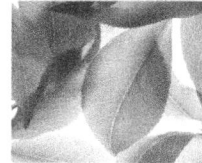 volobor autpat alisim quipis nit iure vendrerit eugait ing et ad magnim amconse min ulla corper in heniat accum am dipit lutatuero od. Aute duisim zzriusto elit illut nismodo uptat, quis am veliquisi. Lor sequis augait lam vel del ullan velis nulputet utat dit nonsed tionsequat.

...and the text wraps around the graphic automatically.

Reminders

Reminders make it easy to track all your to-dos. Create and organize reminders about shopping lists, work projects, or anything else you want to keep track of. You can pick when and where to get reminders. Create a group to assign tasks shared for a project.

Follow up with the smart list: The smart list automatically categorizes your upcoming reminders into 4 categories. Choose Today to view your scheduled reminders for that day and any reminders overdue. Choose Scheduled to view your reminders with a date and time in a chronological view. Select ALL to view all of your reminders in one place.

Smart Lists keep
reminders organized.

Add a reminder.

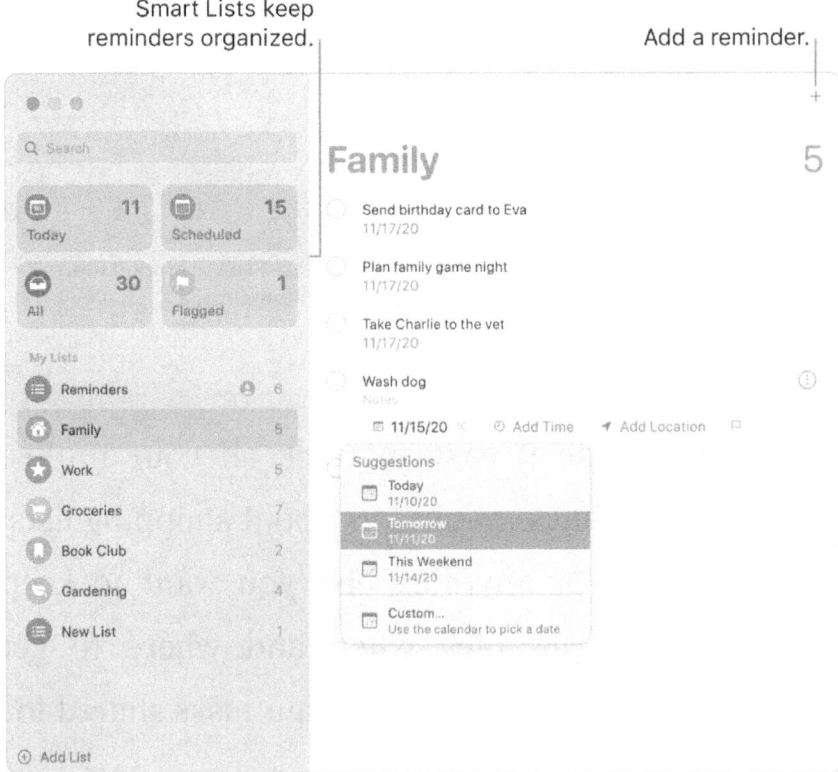

Assign responsibility: Allocate reminders to individuals who you share lists with, so they will be notified. Share tasks and ensure everybody knows their responsibilities. To share a list, select File then click on Share list.

Voice Memos

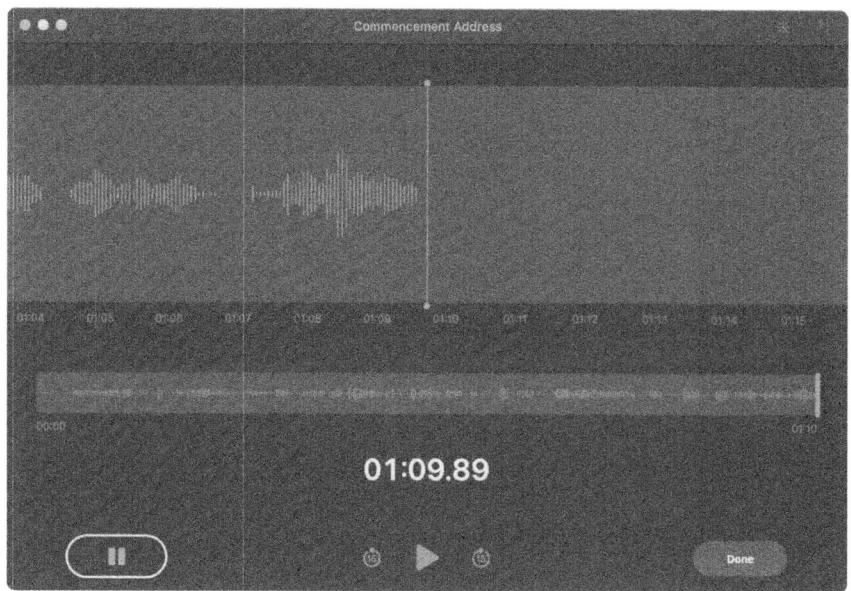

Voice memos make it easy to capture personal reminders, lectures from class, as well as ideas about a song or interviews. With iCloud, you can have access to the voice memos recorded on your iPhone on iMac.

Record from your Mac: Tap on the record icon ● to begin recording, then click on stop when you are done. You can change the name of a recording to make it easier to define. Click on the default name, then type a new one. Tap on Play ▶ to play what you recorded.

Your voice memo on all of your devices: Your voice memo is available on all your devices when you log in with one Apple ID. You can have access to your iPhone or iPad recordings on your iMac.

Use folders

Create folders to assist you in keeping your voice memo in order. Tap on the sidebar icon 🗔 to add a folder and then click the New Folder button at the lower part of the side bar. Type the folder name, and tap on Save. To add your recordings to a folder, hold down click the Options button while dragging your recording to the folder.

Mark recordings as Favorites.

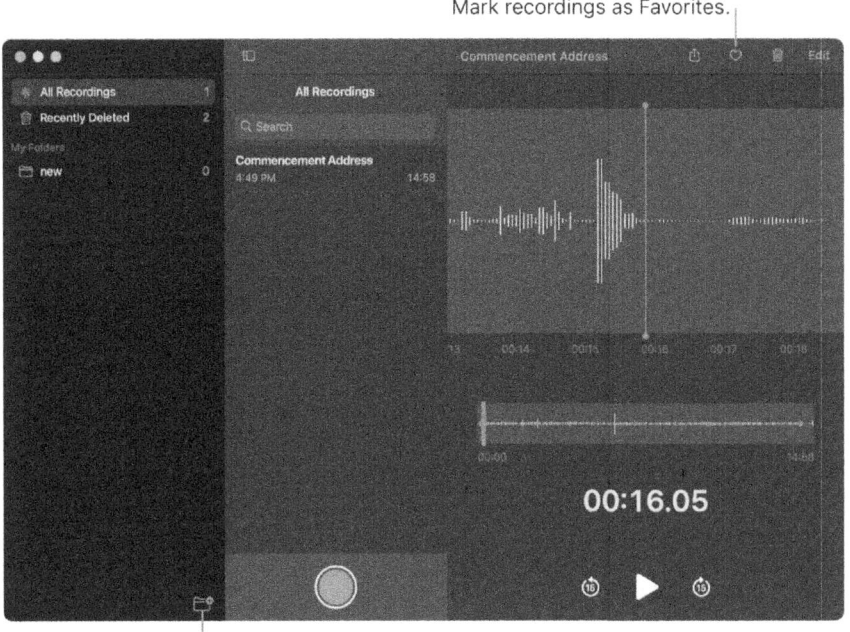

Create new folders to organize your recordings.

Mark any of recording as a Favourite: select any of your recordings then tap on the favourite icon♡ in the tool bar for quick access to the recording later. Click on the sidebar icon⬚, to view all your favorites.

Improve a recording: enhance the quality of the sound in your Voice Memo by reducing the background noise and room clutter. Click on the Edit button at the upper part of the voice memo window, click on the Play button and then click on the Enhance icon ⁂.

Podcast

Use Apple Podcasts to view, subscribe, and listen to your favourite podcasts on your iMac.

Listen Now

Check out the new episodes for subscribed podcasts, and customized offers for your favorite podcasts in one place. Once you sign in using your Apple ID, all podcasts you listen to will be stored in Listen Now.

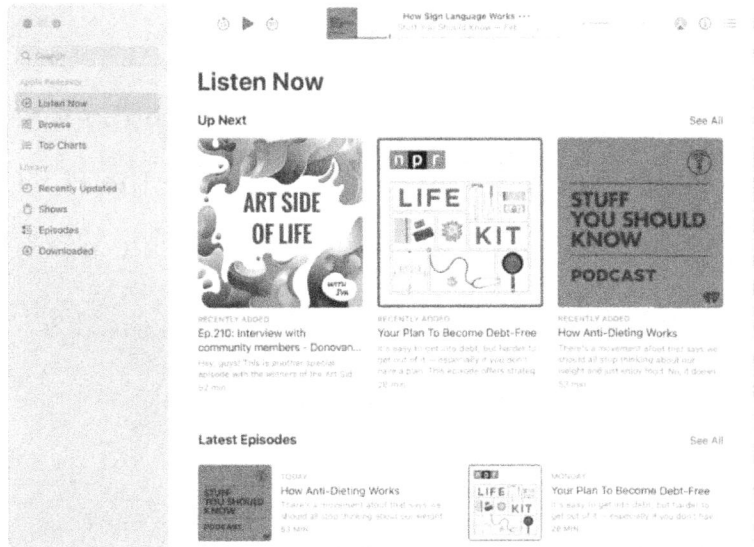

Store episodes to your library

Click the Add button $+$ to store a single episode in your library. Click on the Subscribe button to follow the new episodes of the Podcast. If you want you can click on the Download button ⏬ to listen offline.

Find new podcasts

Look for a new podcast in the Browse segment in the menu bar, or check out trending shows in Top Charts.

Search for a show by the guest or host

When you search for a specific topic or individual, you can find results in shows that they are the Host, shows that you are a guest, and even indicate where they were talked about or discussed.

Messages

It is effortless to connect using messages on your iMac.

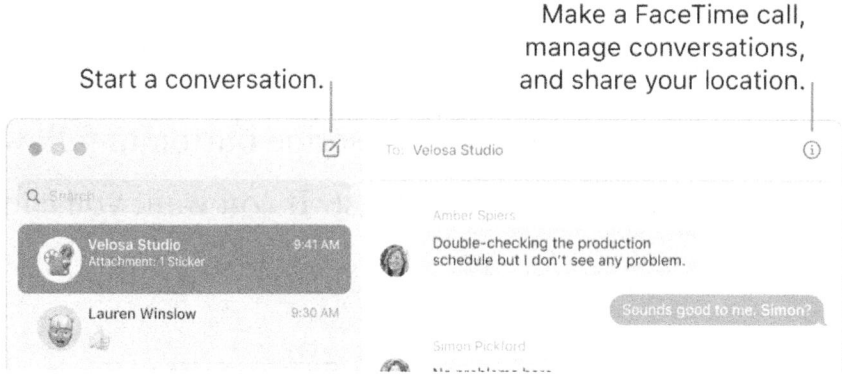

Login using your Apple ID to send and receive messages from anyone with an Apple Watch, iPhone, iPod touch, iPad, or Mac

Pin conversations

To pin a conversation, simply Ctrl-Click on the conversation, then select Pin [name]. or you can swipe right with two of your fingers on the chat sidebar, and then click the Pin icon.

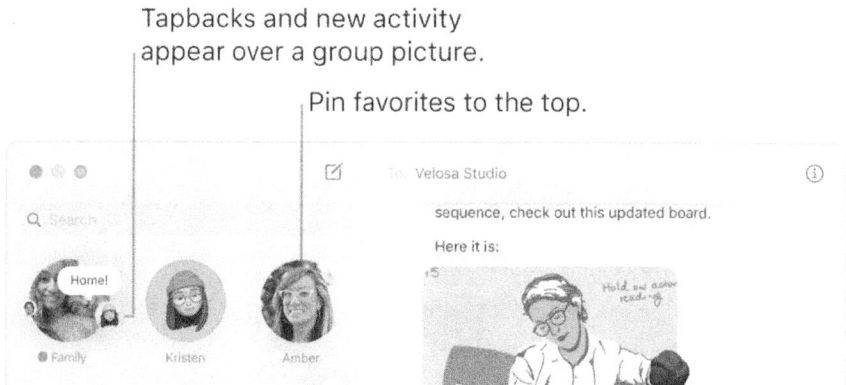

Manage group discussions

In a group chat, you can send a message to someone directly by typing the@ sign before the person's name.

Make the messages interesting

Enhance conversations by responding to messages using Tapbacks, GIF notifications, or special effects. To add special effects or GIF, tap on the Effect icon , select image # or messages effect, and tap on the effect that appeals to you.

Add a photo, sticker, video, or effect.

- Photos
- Memoji Stickers
- #images
- Message Effects

Send a memoji sticker

If you want to send a Memoji sticker in a conversation, click the effect icon, Tap on the Memoji Sticker, and then click the one that might define your mood.

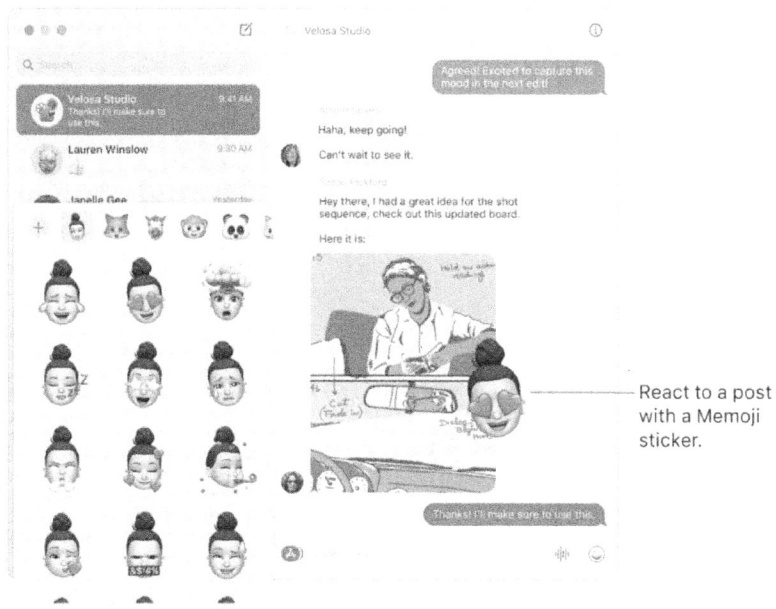

React to a post with a Memoji sticker.

Create your memoji: Choose skin tones, hairstyles, and colors, looks, etc. To create your memoji simply tap on the Effect button then choose the memoji sticker icon after that click on the Add icon ⁺ , then adhere to the directives on the screen to personalize your Memoji, after creating your memoji click on done.

Upload files, photos, or videos: In the conversation, click on the effects icon, click on photo, and then click on a picture to add the picture.

Find My

Utilize the Find My application to find your Apple devices, family, friends, and your personal stuff in one application.

Share location with your friends: In the list of people list, click on the **Share my location** button to tell your friends and relatives where you are

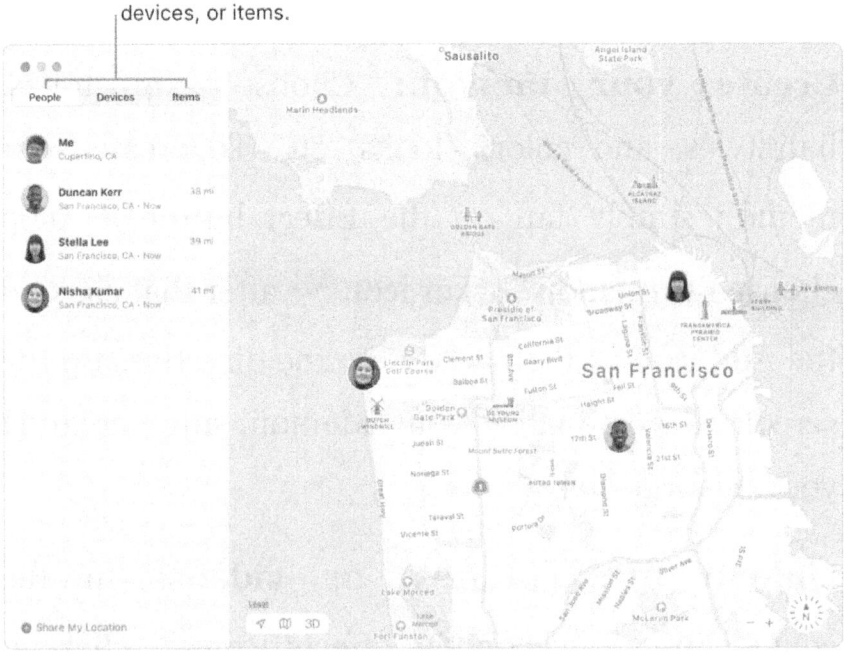

Locate a missing device: Use the Find My application to find and secure any missing Apple Watch, iPod touch, iPad, Mac, iPhone, or AirPods. Click on any device in the Devices catalog to find it on the map. Click the info icon ⓘ to play a sound on the missing device to help you look for it, you can even mark the device as lost so that others can help you look for the device.

Find devices even if they are not online: Find My makes use of Bluetooth signals from other Apple devices near the missing device to find your device when it's not connected to Wi-Fi or a mobile network. These signals are encrypted & anonymous and help you find your device.

Look for everyday items: Attach an Airtag to your items like your key to find it quickly. Configure it with your iPadOS device or iOS device. To find a device with your iMac, click on the Item tab to see the items, and tap on an item in the catalog to see its location in maps. If the item is not found, you can see the location it was seen last and get an alert when it can be located. You can also activate Lost Mode for the item that contains a message and a phone number.

Apple TV

Watch movies and TV shows channels on the Apple TV application. Purchase or rent videos, subscribe to the channel, and start to watch from the part you stopped last time from any of the Apple devices you own.

Watch Now: Keep an eye on your streaming channels and watch movies or TV shows with Watch Now.

Up Next: You will find movies or TV shows, movies and that you are watching, and also the shows you have added to the queue in Up Next. In the Up Next segment, click on the Add to put a movie or show in the list

Buy, rent or subscribe: Once you find the movie or series you want to watch, you can buy or rent it. Your subscribed channels are available on your Apple devices.

Choose items from your library: Click on Library to view all the movies and TV shows that have been downloaded or bought, categorized by genre. Simply tap on the video to start watching.

Maps

Open or close
the sidebar.

Show or hide directions.

Show your current location.

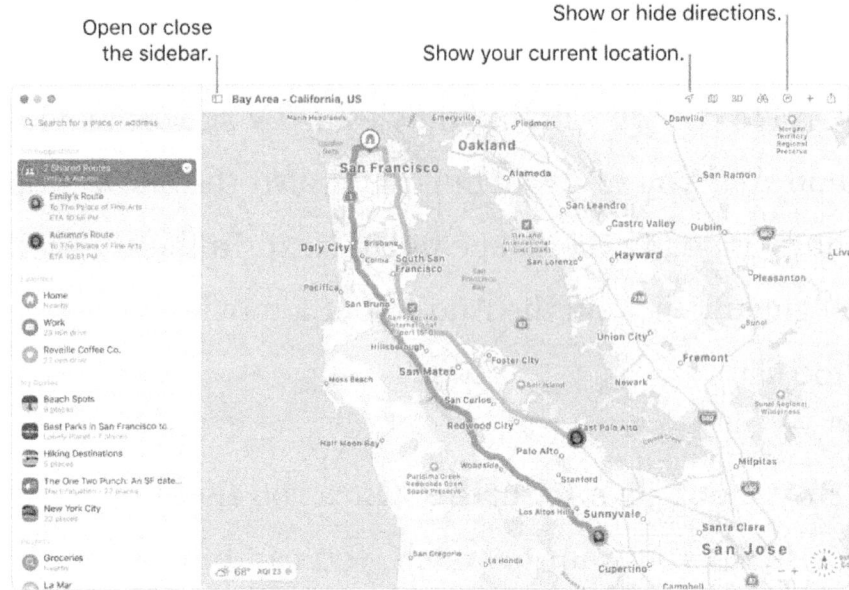

See locations and receive directions with a map or satellite image. Receive recommendations for the best places to go in town with Apple's Guides.

Find a new place with Apple guides: Maps give you directions from trusted brands and partners to help you find the best places to eat, shop, and explore in the world. You can get updates and save these guides when new places get added.

Create your own guide: You can create guides to your favourite places and share them with your friends and relatives. To create a guide, Hover your cursor to My Guides In the side bar, click on the Add icon⊕ on the right, and then ctrl-click on the new guide to find the options menu.

Tour in 3D: Tap on the Look Around icon👓 to explore in 3D as you tour through the streets.

Public transportation

The maps application provides public transportation info for selected cities. Click on a location on the sidebar and click the Transit icon🚊 to get tips on travel routes and the average travel time.

FACETIME

Utilize the FaceTime application to make video and voice calls with your iMac. You can call 32 people with FaceTime Group calls.

FaceTime someone

Enter a name, phone
number, or email address.

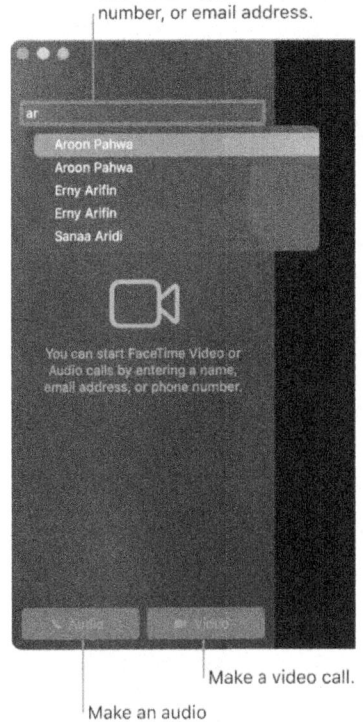

Make a video call.

Make an audio
or phone call.

You can FaceTime people using an iMac, iOS, or iPadOS devices. FaceTime calls utilize Wi-Fi or cellular data.

❖ Sign in to FaceTime on your iMac and ensure FaceTime is activated.

❖ In the search box at the upper part of the FaceTime window, type an e-mail address or a phone number of the individual you plan to call. Press the return button.

❖ Tap on the Video option ▭◁ or the audio icon ☏ to begin the FaceTime call.

Make a Group FaceTime call

1. In the search box in the upper part of the window, type the number or e-mail of the individual you plan on calling. Press the return button.

2. Repeat step 1 till the participants are completely listed.

3. Press the Video call icon or the audio call icon to begin the FaceTime call.

Everybody participating in the call shows up in a tile on your display. When someone speaks, the person's tile moves forward. Tiles that do not fit the screen appear in the sequence below the screen. Scroll down the line to find a participant you do not see.

Tip: If you do not want the tile of the individual talking to be enlarged, you can disable it in the FaceTime options. Select FaceTime then click on preferences..., click on Settings, and disable **Speaking under Automatic Prominence**.

Add more individual to the call

While on a call, you can add more individuals to the call (up to 32 individuals) even if you did not begin start the call.

- While the call is going on, click on the sidebar button ⬚.
- Click on the Add person icon ⊕, then type the email address or phone number of the individual you plan on calling.
- Click on the Add button.

Leave a call

To end a call, do any of the below:

- End the voice call: In the notification, press the End key ◠.
- End a video call: press the Call End button ⊗.

After leaving the FaceTime Group call, all participants continue the call till they all leave. Click on the join Video icon ◌ to be part of the call again.

Take live pictures

You can snap a live picture of any of the people participating in the call to capture a moment from the call. You both receive an alert that the picture was captured and the photo is uploaded directly to the Photo Library. Everyone on the call may have to set the FaceTime option to allow live photos before taking pictures.

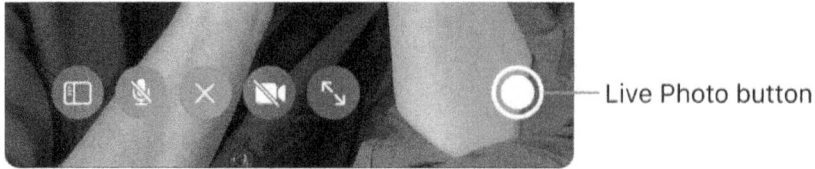

Live Photo button

Setup FaceTime for live pictures

❖ In the FaceTime application on your iMac, select FaceTime then click on preferences and click on Settings.

❖ Choose the **Allow live images to be taken during video calls** checkbox.

After selecting this option, you are also letting others snap live pictures of you.

Setup photos for FaceTime live pictures

The Photo application does not need to be open when you take a live picture, but you must have opened the application at least once to save pictures in the library.

❖ Launch the Photos application on your iMac if you haven't already.

Take a live picture

❖ Do any of the below during a FaceTime video call on:

- In a single person call: Select the FaceTime window.

- In a group call: click on the tile of the individual two times.

❖ Tap on the Live Picture icon ◎ .

The picture would be available on the Photo application

SAFARI

Safari is the quickest and most effective way to access the Internet on your iMac. The start page can be customized to include your favorite images and sections you want to view – which include iCloud charts, Favorites, your playlists, Siri suggestions, frequently accessed sites, & privacy reports. You can get quick translations of websites in other languages.

Personalize the Safari start page

You can place everything from the internet that is very important to you in a convenient place, the start page.

❖ In the Safari application on your iMac, select Bookmarks> display Start page.

❖ Click the Views icon ⚌ in the lower-right part of the page.

❖ Choose the things you want for the Start Page from the list.

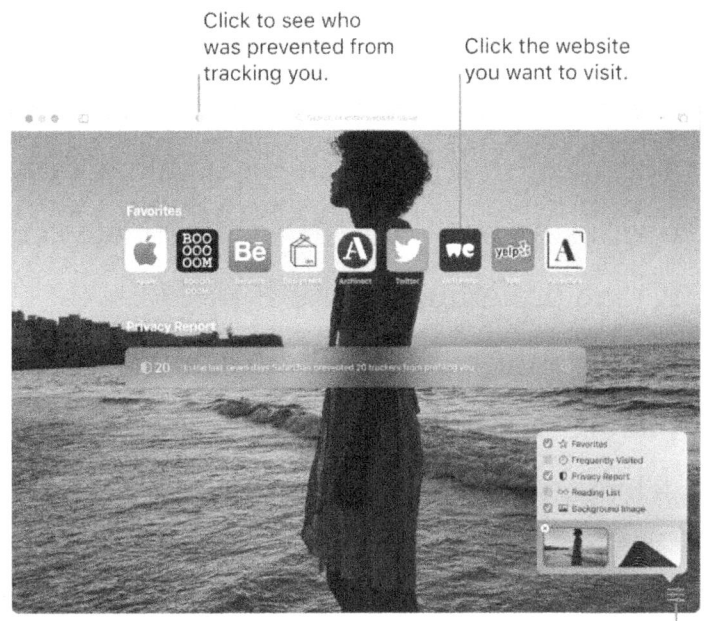

Click to see who was prevented from tracking you.

Click the website you want to visit.

Click to customize the Start Page.

- Favorite: sites you have added as favourites.
- Frequent Visits: Frequently or recently visited pages.
- Privacy Report: Summary, you can click if you need details about sites that were prevented from tracking you.

- Siri Tips.

- Reading list: pages you have added to your reading list.

- iCloud Tabs: Web pages open on your other Apple devices.

  You need to login to all the Apple devices you own using one Apple ID and activate safari in iCloud preferences.

- Background Picture: You can select a given picture or you can tap on the Add button to select any of your images.

Translate a page

❖ Navigate to the website you plan to translate.

  If the site can be translated, Smart Search displays the Translate button .

❖ Click on the translate key , and then select a language.

  If you think the translation should be improved, click the Translate button, and then select the report translation issue button. The translation would be sent to Apple for review.

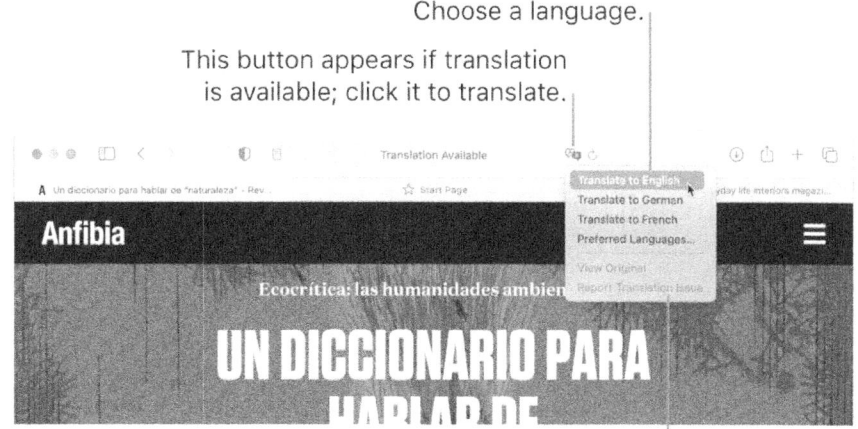

Choose a language.

This button appears if translation is available; click it to translate.

Tell Apple the current translation might need improvement.

Download extension to personalize Safari

You can install Safari extensions to personalize the performance of your browser. For example, extensions can give safari access to features in other applications, and more. The Mac Application Store is the most reliable and easy way to find and install extensions. The extensions get reviewed by Apple and are automatically updated when an automatic update is selected from the App Store preferences.

❖ In the Safari application on your iMac, select Safari then click on Safari extensions and browse for available extensions.

❖ If you find the extension you are looking for, click on the Get or Price button, and click the button to install or purchase the extension.

Manage your extensions

❖ In the Safari application on your iMac, select Safari then click on preferences and click on the Extension button.

❖ Do any of the below:

- Enable or disable extensions: check or disable the extension check box.

- Change a setting for an extension: choose the extension, then unselect or select the setting.

- Remove extension: Select the extension and click the uninstall button. Alternatively, delete the application that contains the extension.

Bookmark a webpage

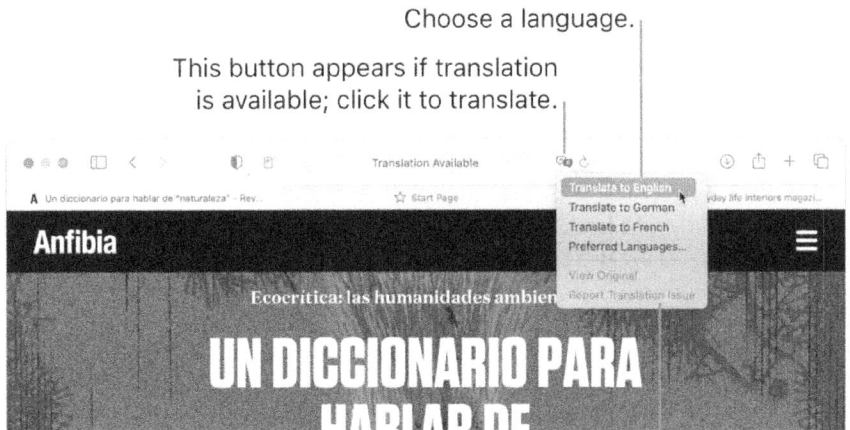

Choose a language.

This button appears if translation
is available; click it to translate.

Tell Apple the current translation
might need improvement.

❖ Go to the page you want to bookmark.

❖ Tap on Share in the toolbar, select Add
Bookmark.

❖ Select where to add the bookmark and name it if
you want

• Add this page: Tap on the drop-down menu
and select a folder.

- Edit the bookmark: Enter a short name that will help in identifying the page.
- Add a comment: Add more information about the website as an additional reminder.

❖ Click Add.

Find the bookmark

❖ In the Safari application, click on the Sidebar icon ▭ on the tool bar, and then click on the Bookmark icon ▭.

❖ Type the bookmark name in the search field in the side bar.

Manage your reading list

To save web pages fast so that you can read them some other time even when you are not connected to the internet, just add them to your Reading List.

In the Safari application, do any of the below:

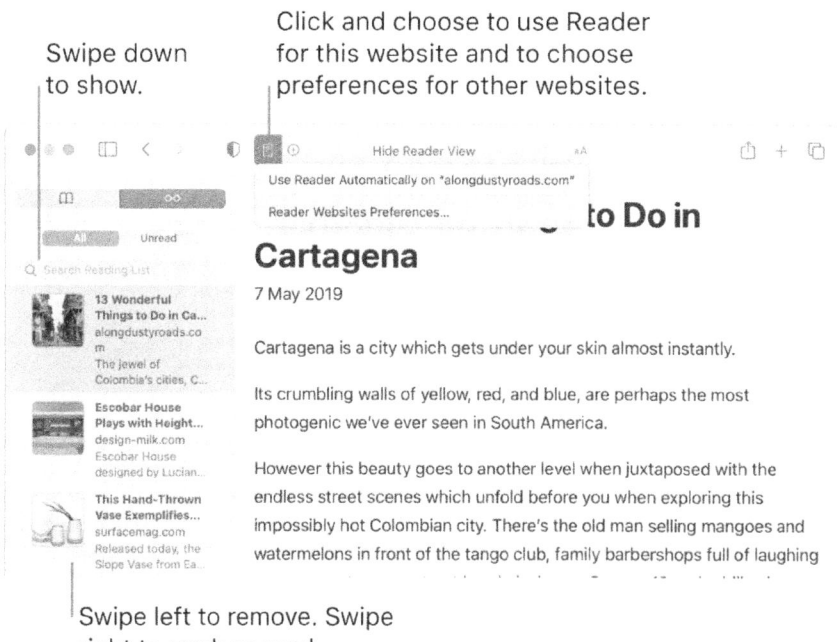

Swipe down to show.

Click and choose to use Reader for this website and to choose preferences for other websites.

Swipe left to remove. Swipe right to mark as read.

❖ Add a webpage to your list: click on the one-step Add icon ⊕ on the left side of the search box.

❖ Display or Hide the reading List: Click on the Side bar icon ▢ to the tool bar, then click on the reading list icon ∞ on top of the side bar. To conceal the list, tap on the sidebar icon once more.

❖ Store a page tour reading list: ctrl-click the page summary on the side bar, then select Save

Offline. Or, swipe to the left over the page summary, and tap on Save Offline.

❖ Erase a webpage from your list: Ctrl-Click the page summary on the side bar, then select the Remove item icon.

Pin a site

Pin frequently visited sites for easy access. The sites you pin are placed on the left part of the tab bar.

Pinned sites stay on the left side of your tab bar.

Drag a pinned site right to unpin it.

Drag a tab left to pin the site.

❖ In the Safari application, drag the site tab to the left part of the tab bar to pin it.

You can also select a Window then tap on the Pin tab or ctrl-click on a tab, then select Pin Tab. To unpin a site simply ctrl-click on the pinned site then select the Unpin Tab option

ICLOUD

iCloud safely saves your applications, music, documents, videos, pictures, etc on all your devices. With iCloud, you can share places, calendars, photos, and more with your friends and family easily. You have to login using your Apple ID to setup iCloud on your Mac.

Setup iCloud features

Once you log in to your Apple ID preference, you can choose which iCloud service you want to use.

Note: to setup message in iCloud so as to be able to share your messages across all your Apple devices, launch message on your iMac, select Messages then tap on preferences, after that click on iMessage, then select Enable Messages in the iCloud checkbox,

❖ On your iMac, select the Apple logo 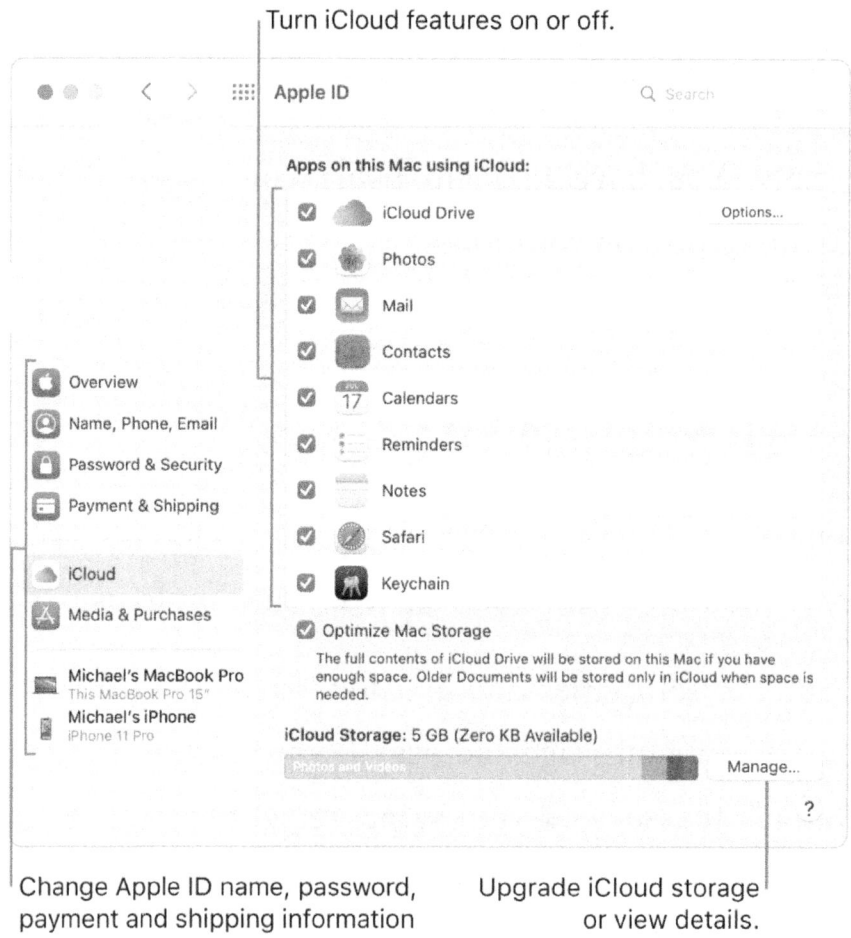 then click on systems preferences…, click on Apple ID, and then choose iCloud in the sidebar.

Turn iCloud features on or off.

Apple ID   Q Search

Apps on this Mac using iCloud:

☑ ☁ iCloud Drive   Options…

☑ 🌼 Photos

☑ ✉ Mail

☑ 📇 Contacts

☑ 17 Calendars

☑ ⁝ Reminders

☑ ▭ Notes

☑ 🧭 Safari

☑ 🐾 Keychain

☑ Optimize Mac Storage

The full contents of iCloud Drive will be stored on this Mac if you have enough space. Older Documents will be stored only in iCloud when space is needed.

iCloud Storage: 5 GB (Zero KB Available)

Photos and Videos   Manage…

?

Overview
Name, Phone, Email
Password & Security
Payment & Shipping

iCloud
Media & Purchases

Michael's MacBook Pro
This MacBook Pro 15"
Michael's iPhone
iPhone 11 Pro

Change Apple ID name, password, payment and shipping information and more.

Upgrade iCloud storage or view details.

❖ Choose the application whose iCloud features you plan to utilize. Remove any iCloud application you don't want to use by deselecting it.

Some features have additional settings, which you can change when you click on Options or detail next to the feature name when the feature is activated.

Manage your iCloud storage

When you sign in to your Apple ID and activate your iCloud preferences, you will get 5 GB of free storage. If you run out of storage space, you can upgrade it to have more space. You can also remove saved items to get more space.

❖ On your iMac, select the Apple menu, click on systems preferences, then tap on the Apple ID, and choose iCloud in the side bar.

❖ Tap on manage, then do any of the below:

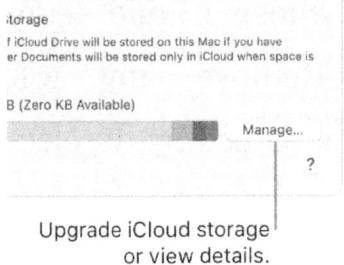

storage

f iCloud Drive will be stored on this Mac if you have
er Documents will be stored only in iCloud when space is

B (Zero KB Available)

Manage...

?

Upgrade iCloud storage
or view details.

❖ Upgrade your storage space

❖ See how an application or features is making use of storage

❖ Disable Siri and remove Siri-related information.

SIRI

You can talk to Siri on your iMac and ask Siri to perform a task for you. For instance, you can view files, organize meetings, change your preferences, receive replies, send messages, send calls, and add items to your calendar. To utilize Siri, your iMac has to be connected to the Internet.

Activate Siri

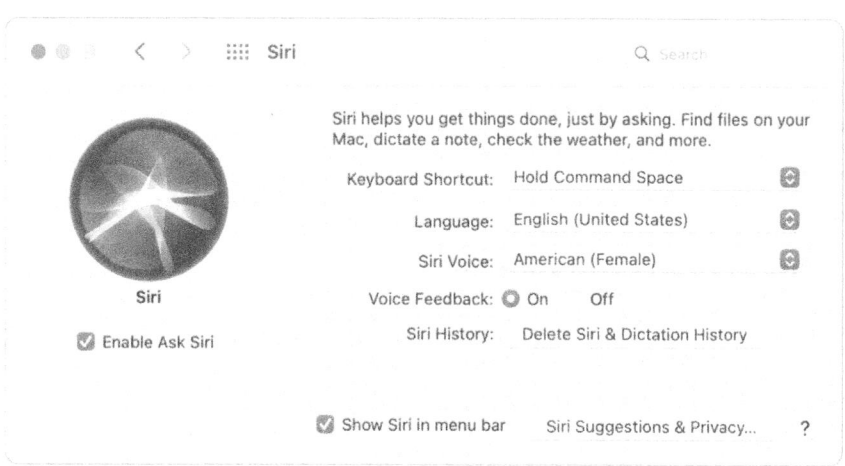

Launch systems preferences, click on Siri, and adjust the options. If you activated Siri while setting up your device, press and hold the Cmd-Space bar combination to launch Siri. Or In System Preference, click on Enable Ask To Siri. You can also set up other options to use it, such as voice & language to utilize and whether to display Siri in the menu bar.

Talk to Siri

Hold down the Command-Space bar button (or say "Hey Siri" if you activated this feature) and start talking.

Change Siri's voice

Click on Siri in the systems preferences..., select a voice for Siri from the Siri voice menu.

APPLE PAY

With Apple Pay on IMac, you can make easier, more secure purchases from sites. When you make use of Apple Pay, your Apple Cards, and other credit or debit cards are never distributed or stored to merchants by Apple. When shopping online using Safari, look for the Apple Pay payment option. Confirm that you purchased with the magic key using Touch ID.

Setup Apple Pay

❖ On your iMac with Touch ID keyboard, enter System Preferences> Wallet and Apple Pay.
❖ Click on the Add Card button.
❖ Adhere to the directions on your screen to add a new card.

Buy things using Touch ID

Click on the Apple Pay icon on the site, then confirm the payment you are making with your Touch ID on your keyboard.

TIPS AND TRICKS

Play sound on startup options

Now you can choose whether or not your iMac would play the custom startup chime or not. Launch System Preferences... then click on Sound, and tick the checkbox beside Play sound on startup.

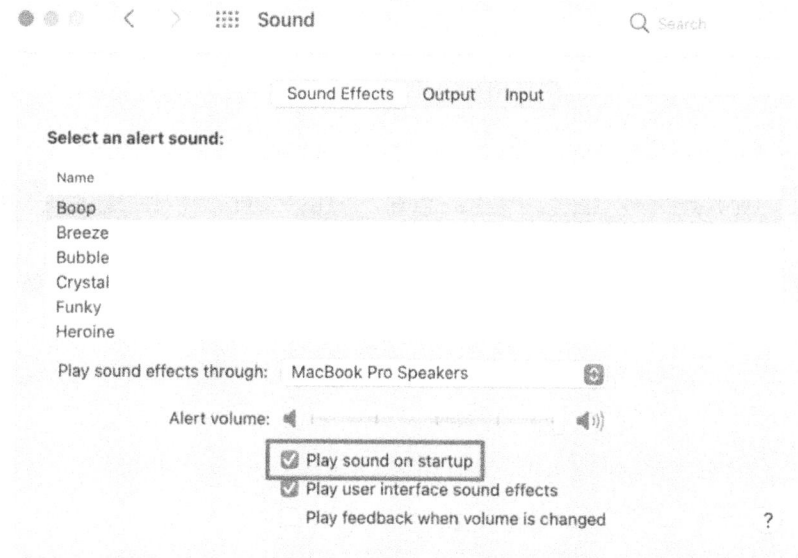

Control Wallpaper Tinting in window

In Big Sur, the windows are colored based on the colour of the desktop screensaver. If you do not want it, you can disable the colored tinting of windows, simply head over to the systems preferences... -> General and deselect the checkbox beside **Allow wallpaper tinting in windows**

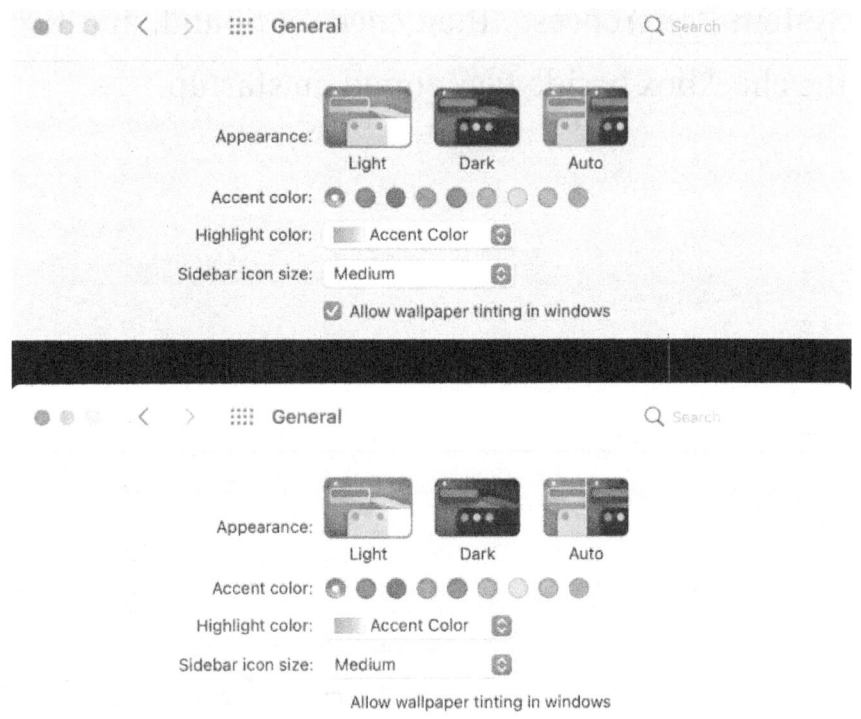

Hear what you type

In System Preferences, the speech segment in the Accessibility has been given a new name which is Spoken Content, and there is a new feature known as **Speak typing Responses**, once activated it will speak out what you are typing as you type it.

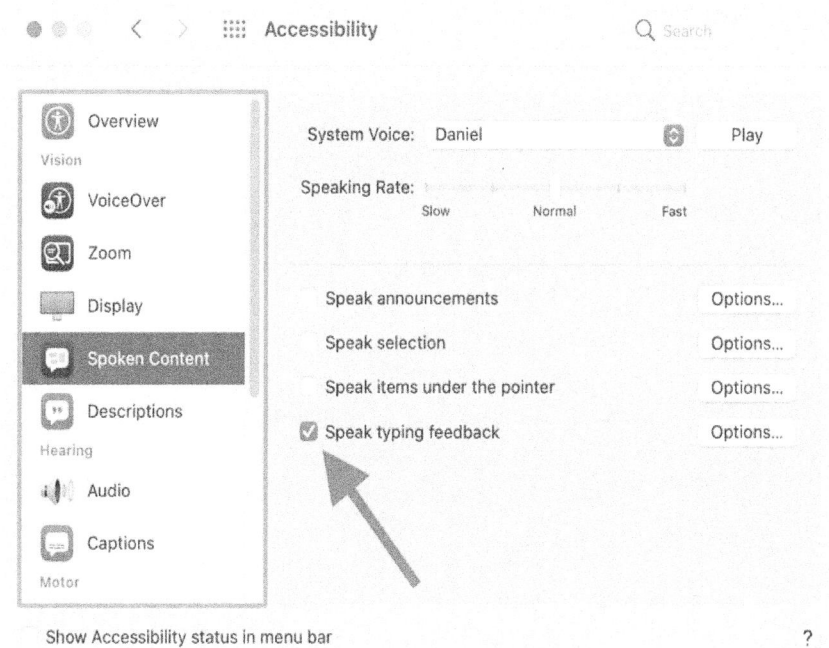

Hide the menu bar

On macOS 11, Apple has released an option that allows you to conceal the desktop menu bar. This feature can be found in the Dock and Menu segment of Systems Preferences.

To setup the menu bar to hide and display whenever you hover the pointer to the top of your display, tick the **Automatically display and hide the menu bar** checkbox

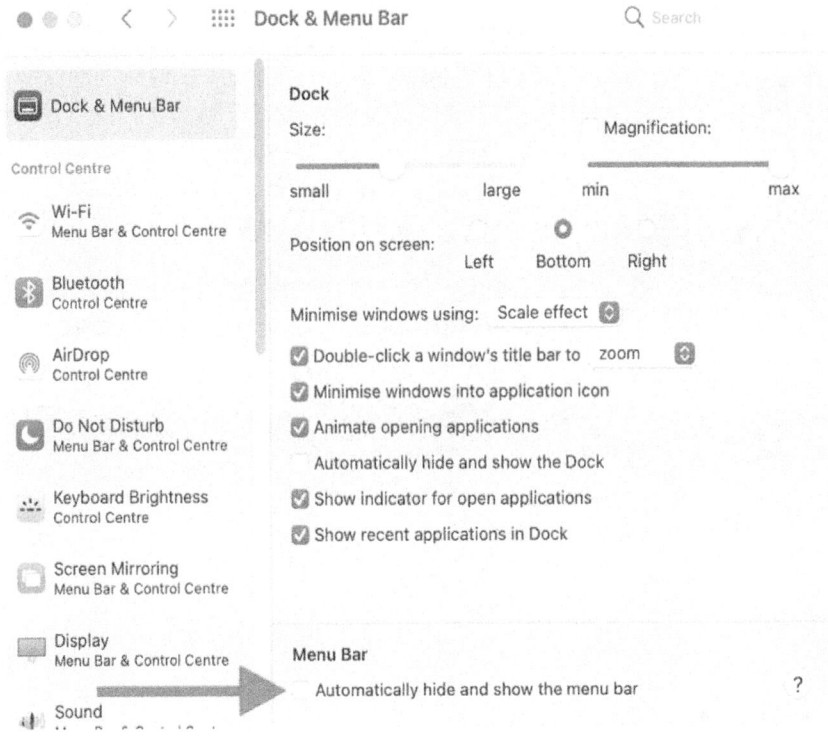

Personalize the control center

In System Preferences, the Dock and Menu Bar segment allows you to select what is found in the Control Center. You can Enable & disable some controls like AirDrop, Bluetooth, Wi-Fi, DND, and many more.

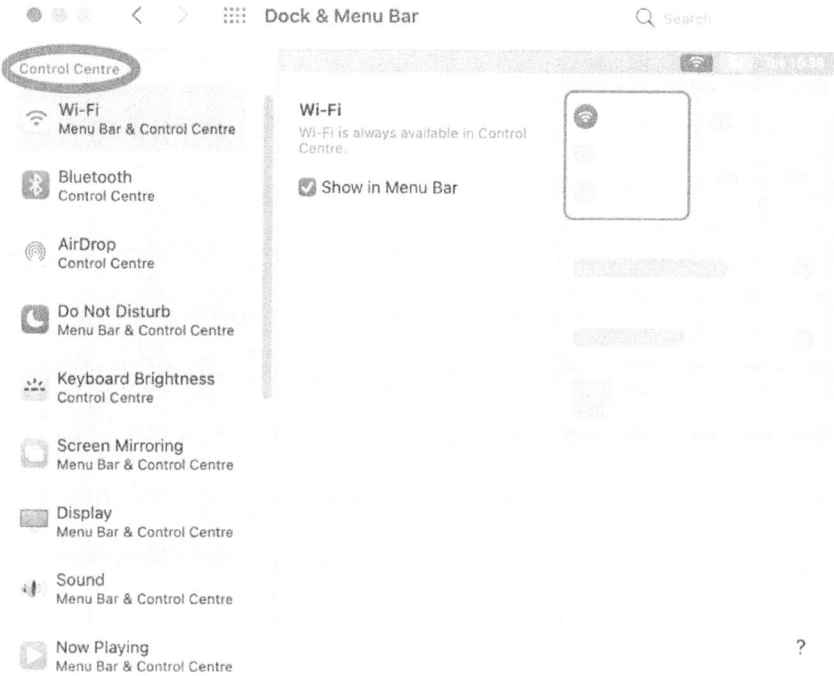

Import passcodes & settings from Chrome

Safari allows you to transfer passcodes and setting from Chrome, as well as your bookmark & history.

You can find the setting in the Safari menu bar under File -> Import from -> Google Chrome

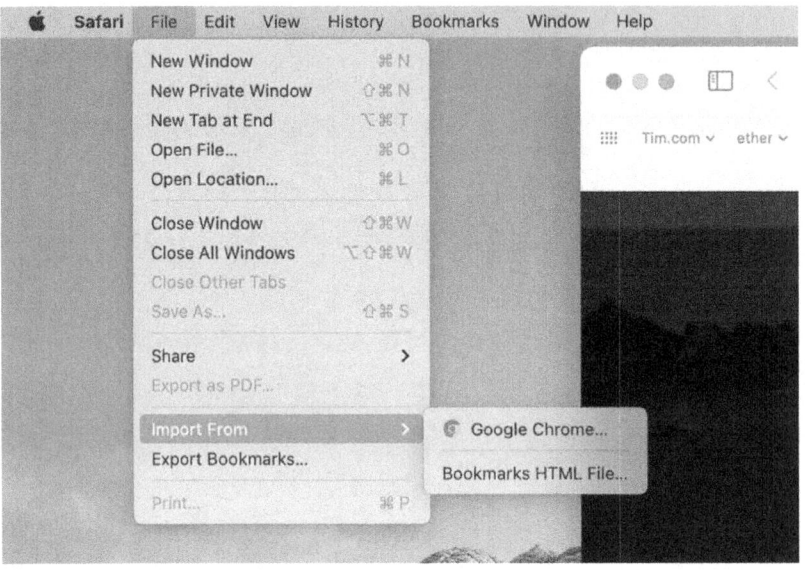

New wallpaper

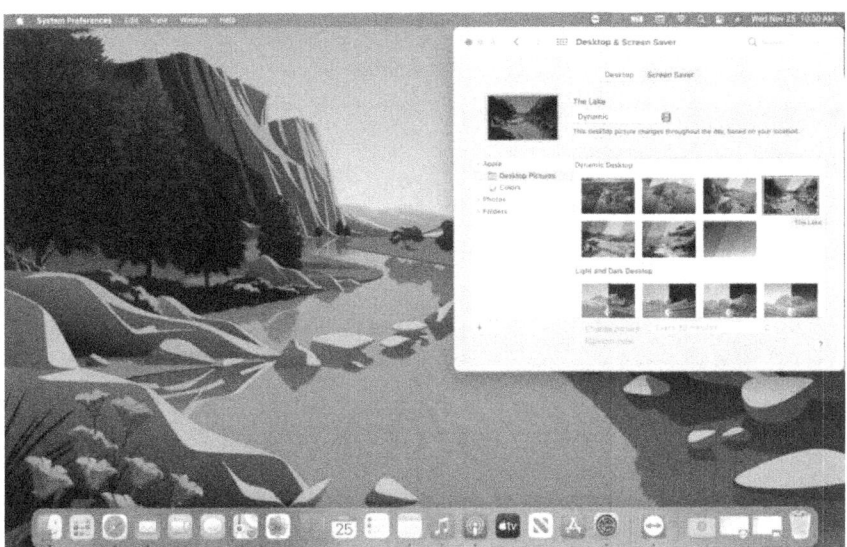

Big Sur features about 40 new wallpapers. You can find these new wallpapers in system preferences-> Desktop and screen savers

Resize widgets

The notification center now has redesigned widgets. Most of the widgets can be resized, simply Right-click the widget then select one of the sizes (Large, Medium, or Small).

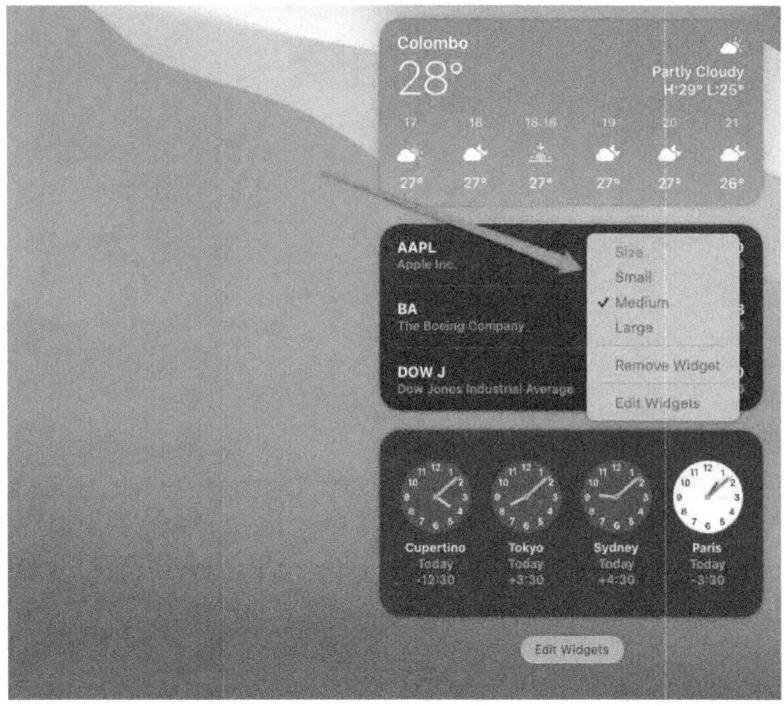

Change Accent to multi-colored

macOS Big Sur allows software developers to define their accent colors. This is because of a new accent colour scheme known as "multi-colored". Go to System Preferences> General and tap on the accent radio button on the left to activate multicolor.

Once you do so, the applications would show a variety of accent colours as planned by the developers.

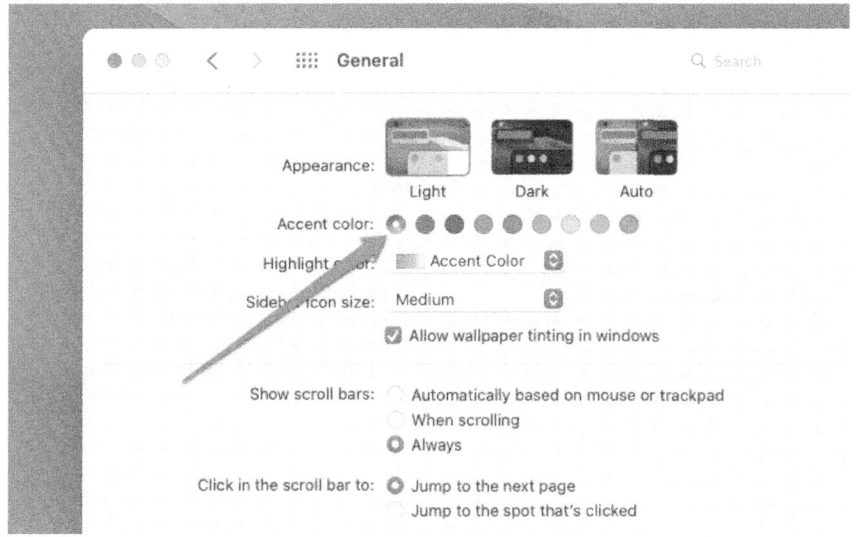

Made in the USA
Coppell, TX
08 March 2022